Ocean Liner

Collectibles

Myra Yellin Outwater

Photography by Eric Boe Outwater

4880 Lower Valley Rd. Atglen, PA 19310 USA

Dedication

To my husband Eric, the perfect shipmate and travel companion, who makes every trip the best adventure of all. Two years ago, as he became an avid collector himself, he suggested that we write a book about collectibles. It is because of his photography skills that we have such a beautiful product.

To my son, Alexander Goldfarb, whose love of QE2 was the reason for two crossings and for the presence in our library of a growing number of "ship" books. Alexander's enthusiasm led to the acquisition of a White Star dinner plate, a complete set of china from a QE2, a French Line ashtray, a lithograph of Cunard's Umbria, and eventually this book.

To Charlie Schalebaum, who helped me ferret out so many of my treasures and gave me the courage and the reason to buy, buy, and buy. He also allowed us access to his own collection.

To Paul Mackerer, who turned disaster into beauty. When my basement flooded, he convinced me to rebuild it to look like a cabin on the Normandie. It was Paul who helped organize our collection so that others could enjoy it and relive past voyages.

Finally, this book is dedicated to all those ship buffs who collect "ship stuff." It is also dedicated to all those armchair travelers, whose bodies may be landlocked, but whose imaginations still roam freely at sea.

Designed by Bonnie M. Hensley
Layout by Randy L. Hensley
Type set in Seagull Hv BT/Times New Roman

ISBN: 0-7643-0581-6
Printed in China
1 2 3 4

Published by Schiffer Publishing Ltd.
4880 Lower Valley Road
Atglen, PA 19310
Phone: (610) 593-1777; Fax: (610) 593-2002
E-mail: Schifferbk@aol.com

In Europe Schiffer books are distributed by
Bushwood Books
6 Marksbury Avenue Kew Gardens
Surrey TW9 4JF England
Phone: 44 (0) 181 392-8585; Fax: 44 (0) 181 392-9876
E-mail: Bushwd@aol.com

Please write for a free catalog.
This book may be purchased from the publisher.
Please include $3.95 for shipping. Please try your bookstore first.
We are interested in hearing from authors with book ideas on related subjects.

Table of Contents

Acknowledgments

To Harold Goldfarb, who first showed me that the QE2 was the only way to cross.

To the Cunard Line, the Bergen Line, the Peter Deilmann EuropAmerica Cruises.

To Richard Faber.

To Ronald Warwick, Captain of QE2, and his wife Kim, Captain Tore Lura and Gerard Eltzner of the Royal Viking Sun, and Volker Roloff of the Vistafjord.

To Priscilla Hoye, Eileen Dailey, Linda Ragsdale and Julie Davis of Cunard. To Ron Santangelo and Lucille Hoshabjian of Peter Deilmann EuropAmerica Cruises. To Karen Schimmel of the Bergen Line. To Maureen Ryan, David Greenwell, and Peter Warwick of QE2.

Very special thanks to Ole Bertilsen, who spent so many hours showing us the china of the QE2 and explaining the history of her logos.

Thanks to all those stewards, waiters, waitresses, and sommeliers who gave us so many wonderful memories of days at sea in the Atlantic, Pacific, and Indian oceans and the North, Red, and Mediterranean seas.

Thank you to David Gaskill for your zeal in making this book letter perfect.

Though we have found bits and pieces of information on ocean-liner collectibles in most price guides, no other book has systematically categorized them as a whole. We owe a lot to all the work and research done by so many before us, like John Maxtone-Graham, William Miller, Frank Braynard, and Walter Lord.

Introduction

At Sea, Or Why Collect?

The sea can be a friend or a foe. In the 1920s, a giant wave struck down on the Bremen so fiercely that the captain had to heave to in mid-Atlantic and the ship's arrival in port was delayed three days.

Many years later, on the morning of September 11, 1995, QE2 was struck so hard by a ninety-five-foot "rogue wave" that the entire ship shuddered.

The ocean has always been a mysterious magnet drawing men and women to cross its boundaries.

In his book *Life on the Mississippi*, Mark Twain wrote: "The face of the river, in time, became a wonderful book... and it was not a book to be read once and thrown aside, for it had a new story to tell every day."

It is this story that has intrigued sailors, ship buffs, and armchair travelers. Like the rivers, the oceans of this world have been a source of wonder, fascination, and adventure since the beginning of civilization.

While to many it has been man's foe, a barrier to be crossed, to others it has been man's friend, connecting families and communities, strengthening the economy, providing food and natural protection. And if at times oceans conjure up visions of raging seas and arduous long crossings, at other times they also bring to mind scenes of people engaged in commerce and play, oceangoing barges loaded with produce, fishermen crouched on the banks of outlets or on rock strewn quays, fishing side by side with graceful, dabbling ducks, swooping seagulls, and soaring murres, gannets, and cormorants.

While many love the sight of rolling waves and limitless horizons, my favorite view of the ocean is always at night, when there are no other lights but the stars and the moon, and the only sound is the lapping of the waves.

How Much Is It Worth? A Suggested Value Analysis and Price Guide

Ship collectibles increase in value relative to scarcity. Maiden voyage "ship stuff" and memorabilia from final voyages have uniqueness value, as do items from ships no longer in service.

There is no such thing as the average ship buff. There are those who still travel regularly by sea; there are the "romantics" who just love any touch of a ship at sea, and there are the dreamers who sit at home and experience the sea vicariously.

Unlike other collectible fields, age is not a determinant of value for ocean-liner buffs. Some ships have more allure than others to collectors such as the disaster ships the Titanic, the Lusitania, the Morro Castle, and the Andrea Doria. Other collectors specialize in shipping lines such as Cunard, White Star, the French, or the Italian Lines. Others are mesmerized by the charisma of the giants such as the Normandie or the Cunard Queens.

On one crossing on the Raffaello, I mentioned the name of the Normandie to a fellow passenger. The next day he returned to the dining room with a stack of well-worn photographs. As he showed me pictures of the deck, the crew, and the various public rooms, tears filled his eyes.

Not only are there different kinds of collectors, there are different categories of dealers. Top-of-the-line dealers sell furnishings, Lalique glass, paintings, and lithographs that command hundreds and thousands of dollars. The majority of dealers sell items from $10 menus to $200 plates. The amateurs sell off bits and pieces from $5 to $100.

Unlike other collectible fields, there is no shortage of ocean-liner memorabilia. We have found treasure-troves in old travel albums—seasoned travelers saved everything from menus to passage tickets, from dining room tickets to old bills. We have found unexpected treasures—china, ashtrays, models, playing cards, or paintings—at flea markets, thrift shops, and garage sales.

Some collectors seek objects related to a particular ship that has meaning in their lives. Other collectors collect because, as children they visited, sailed on, or saw the ships docked in New York. In the 1940s, 1950s, and 1960s, before security became such a serious consideration, it was possible to buy a ticket for a few cents and tour the liners in port. Many of the leading collectors and ocean liner historians still remember standing as children, watching the great liners sail up the Hudson, or holding their parents' hands during a visit to the piers.

In the early days of this century, an ocean passage could be booked with the frequency of today's air and rail travel. Each of the great lines maintained a fleet of three to four sister ships, and ships arrived and departed the New York piers daily.

As in all pricing guides for collectibles, value is relative, determined by condition, scarcity, and demand. We have tried to give approximate values, but the final price is always determined in the marketplace, based on what dealers and their customers are willing to pay. Since the market for ocean-liner collectibles is a relatively new field, prices are approximate and do fluctuate.

Many dealers have told us that they do not want a price guide because there is no standard price and many collectibles are one of a kind. Taking this into account, we have tried to give a fair range to our pricing and value analysis. But we offer this caveat to collectors: There is no one price. There is only availability, and when buying pieces for a collection, follow your heart and your pocketbook. There is always an ocean liner collectible in your price range.

Recently we found a wall sculpture from the dining room of the United States on sale for $5,000. Since it was out of our price range, we substituted a unique United States aluminum vase for $200. The beauty of collecting ocean-liner memorabilia is that we could also have bought a piece of the United States magic with $10 for a menu, $30 for a room key or $25 for a water goblet.

A 1995 Christie's auction brought in record prices ranging in the thousands and hundreds of thousands of dollars. Ocean liner collectible dealers report that they can sell out their mail-order catalogs within days.

There is also the tempting possibility that a free stash of mementos lies hidden in a relative's attic, in an old photo album, or in a blanket chest. Treasures are out there at yard sales, flea markets, and in old book shops. The joy of collecting is that it is still an open frontier and there is ship stuff aplenty to be found. Ahoy and good luck!

A Bit of History Sails By, or Get It While It's Still Out There

For those who love the romance of the great ocean liners and mourn their demise from the high seas, the loss is further emphasized by the standardization of today's ship logos. Going, going, gone are the distinctive logos, personalized ship china, playing cards, and decorative menu covers that created a world of floating elegance. Instead, economics have forced ship management to look at future cost savings. One of the first victims was logo-adorned china, ashtrays, glassware, silverware, and artful menu covers.

Ironically, all this comes at a crucial moment in ocean liner history. Never have so few ships crossed the oceans nor have there been so many eager, deep-pocketed collectors and dealers willing to pay what often seem to be astronomical prices for a piece of china from the Queen Mary, a sofa from the Normandie, or a deck chair from the United States. Christie's auctions on ship items bring in thousands of inquiries and sell out catalogs. Swap meets such as the one hosted by the Ocean Liner Society in New York City attract hundreds of smaller collectors, who spend $10 to $150 for spoons, cups, playing cards, cookie tins, postcards, and gala ribbons.

One of the earliest harbingers of change was noted a few years ago on Cunard's flagships. For years Cunard used Wedgwood china ashtrays with the distinctive golden Cunard lion. In recent years, however, these china ashtrays have been replaced in public rooms by plain glass ashtrays minus the logo. To simulate the logo, these glass ashtrays are placed on top of paper cocktail napkins with the ship's logo so that the Cunard lion still shines through.

A 1996 trip on the Vistafjord illustrated how economic constraints have impacted future collectors. On the wall of his small cramped office on the Vistafjord, Hotel Manager Volker Roloff hung three plates—one royal blue, one green, and one white with gold fish along its rim. These three dinner plates represent the past, future, and present of the china used in the Vistafjord dining room.

When Cunard bought the Vistafjord and her sister ship, the Sagafjord, in 1983 from Norwegian American Cruise Lines, the restaurant management found a variety of patterns of tableware in service—silver plate carrying the initials of its former owners, Norwegian American Cruise lines (NAC), Norwegian American Lines (NAL), and the new Cunard logos.

In anticipation of the ship's most recent refurbishing in 1993–94, Cunard decided to phase out the ship's blue china and create a new streamlined design.

The team ordered a special green plate with the Cunard lion on top and a fish border. The green was intended to match the green of the new dining room.

Unfortunately, the green plates never saw service because the green of the prototype clashed with the existing greens in the dining room. It was almost impossible to get the porcelain green to match the carpeting and upholstery greens. So the design team decided to opt for two plates, one a fluted white plate with a gold rim, the other, a white and gold plate with a fish border to be used only for fish courses. It was decided that having a special plate for fish courses added a touch of elegance and enhanced the feel of a luxurious dining room.

In the years to come, further cost savings will have eliminated the gold Cunard lion logo completely and standardized the china throughout the fleet. Ship logos such as the Royal Viking Sun's sea eagle, the Sea Goddess's mermaid, the Vistafjord's Viking ship, and the QE2's lion, still remain on stationary, but the china, glassware, and silverware are becoming logo-free.

It is unclear how these cutbacks will influence future memorabilia hunters. Also, who knows whether these cost-saving measures will affect the aesthetics and romance of shipboard life, particularly in the dining room, and eliminate some of the glamour of the shipboard experience? Whether or not these "unmarked" items will appease the acquisition lust of young collectors is still unknown. But collectors are hopeful that the new line of gift shop items will inaugurate a new era of collectibles.

Assorted Titanic memorabilia.

The Norway in New York City in August 1997.

A card case taken from the Titanic by a disgruntled steward who had been reassigned to the Olympic. $30,000-plus.

More ship stuff from the Compagnie Generale Transatlantique, Raffaello, Queen Mary, Hamburg American HAPAG Cunard and a Canoe perfume bottle in the shape of a sailor.

The sea can be a friend or a foe. In the 1920s, a big wave hit the Bremen, delaying its arrival in New York for three days.

A postcard of the Royal Viking Sun. $1.

This is the first promotional brochure issued by the Swedish America Line for the Stockholm's maiden voyage in 1948. $60. The M.S. Stockholm became famous after her July 26, 1952 collision with the Andrea Doria, which sank after the two ships collided. Since then, Stockholm memorabilia have become desirable collectibles. This small model was sold aboard ship in 1948. $65.

Photographs taken aboard the Normandie by a passenger. $25 each.

Photographs of ships from the Cunard/White Star Line in the 1930s. $25 each.

Photographs of the Normandie and the Lavoisier. $25 each.

A goblet, a menu, a key, and an aluminum vase used on the United States.

A cabin key from the United States. $60.

A menu cover from the United States. $10.

This Bremen ashtray was found in a junk store in Connecticut and cost $2. It has been listed in catalogs for $60. It was a gift item celebrating 100 years for the North German Lloyd shipping line.

A champagne goblet used on the United States with the eagle insignia. $125.

Two chairs and a table used on the Normandie.

Everyone knows someone who has been on an ocean trip and there are treasure-troves of ship stuff hidden away in boxes and trunks in attics. This 1969 menu from the Raffaello was a gift from my aunt, Mrs. Lillian Altman. $15.

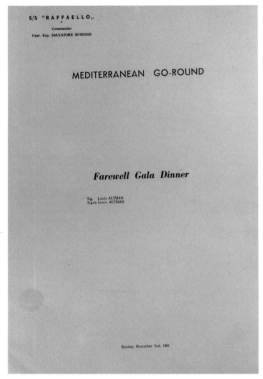

Notice the personalized inscription, Signor and Signorina Louis Altman.

A cabin key from QE2. People want to collect, and the joy of collecting ocean liner stuff is that there is something for every budget. $30.

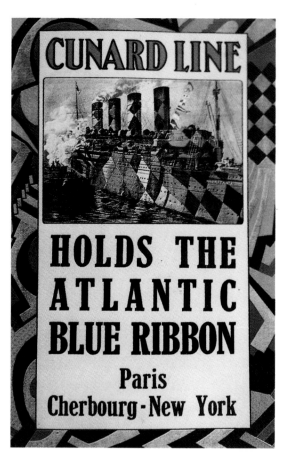

A menu cover from the American President Lines. $10.

The Cunard Mauretania held the Blue Ribbon for years. Speed was one of the biggest selling points in the race to dominate the North Atlantic trade. The Blue Ribbon (also known as the Blue Riband or the Blue Ribband) was given to the fastest ship crossing the Atlantic. The S.S. United States was the last to hold the record.

A menu cover from the American President Lines. $10.

Speed and size were important in selling these liners to the public. This poster for the Hamburg-Amerika Line's Imperator boasts that it is the largest ship in the world. The eagle was placed on the ship's bow to extend its length. Later it was lost, a victim of a North Atlantic storm. While original ship posters sell for thousands of dollars, full-size prints and lithographs of these posters can sell for $50-$350. Postcards sell for $1 and up and can also capture the excitement of the age and be a fascinating collectible for beginners.

A postcard of the QE2 in 1997 after its third refit. $2.

Cunard ashtrays show the changing Cunard lion logo. $25-$30.

The blue and white plate formerly used on Sagafjord and Vistafjord with the Cunard lion. $25.

The white fish plate used on Vistafjord for the fish courses. Notice there is no Cunard lion logo. $25.

The unsuccessful green prototype with the Cunard lion logo. $100, only twelve exist.

Chapter 1

The Ships: Great Floating Palaces of the Seas

Lithographs, Postcards, and Photographs

Oceangoing traffic began primarily as a cargo service. The Black Ball line was one of the earliest American companies to carry transatlantic passengers. In 1839, Samuel Cunard, along with two partners, established the first competitive transatlantic shipping line, the North American Royal Mail Steam Packet Company. Cunard envisioned ships that would not only transport cargo and mail, but passengers from Liverpool to Halifax, Nova Scotia, and Boston.

Cunard was among the first to emphasize passenger safety over speed. He prided himself on the fact that his red-funneled ships ran in all weather. His motto was "Comfort, Safety, and Speed," and his orders to his officers were no racing, no risk-taking, and no ship rivalries.

Within a year his line was the first regularly scheduled transatlantic service and Cunard's ships were sailing from Liverpool to Boston. His 1856 Persia was the first iron-hulled Cunarder. His 1862 China became the first to be driven by a propeller rather than a paddle wheel, and the 1881 Servia had a steel hull and was the first Cunarder to have electric lighting on board. By 1893, the Lucania and the Campania had dispensed with sails completely in favor of twin propellers.

By 1880, Samuel Cunard had bought out his partners and founded what would become the most famous fleet of passenger ships, the Cunard Steamship Company.

For the next one hundred and fifty plus years, the name Cunard would become an enduring presence on the Atlantic Ocean and the company would own or manage more than 200 ships.

The American Collins Line, which was founded in 1850, was the first to challenge Cunard, and for several years offered strong competition. The Collins Line ships—the Atlantic, the Arctic, the Baltic, and the Pacific were the first ships to offer separate smoking room areas, bathrooms, a barbershop, and hot water.

In 1852 and 1854, two more lines, the Anchor Line and the Allan Line, were founded and began to ply the Atlantic. Later the Allan Line would become known as the Canadian Pacific line.

But it would be the French Compagnie Generale Transatlantique, which was founded in 1855, and two German companies—the North German Lloyd Line, founded in 1857, and the Hamburg-Amerika Line, founded in 1862—that would change the history of ocean liners and offer Cunard its strongest competition. The Hamburg American lines would later be known as HAPAG (Hamburg Amerikansche Packetfahrt Actien Gesellschaft).

In 1868, another Englishman, Thomas Ismay, bought the assets of a bankrupt Australian shipping company, the White Star Line.

By the late 1890s, the great age of transatlantic passenger service began in earnest as England and Germany began a battle for supremacy of the Atlantic trade. The two countries continued to launch a competitive series of ships, each more luxurious and opulent than the one before. This race continued until the beginning of World War I, when many of these passenger ships were converted for wartime use.

The first great twentieth century ocean liner was the White Star's Oceanic. In 1899, the Oceanic was considered the greatest and most elaborately fitted vessel ever built. The White Star line, which was registered under the corporate name Oceanic Steamer Navigation Company, Ltd. in 1869, became one of Cunard's biggest rivals.

In 1901, American financier J. P. Morgan bought an interest in the White Star line for $10 million. For years Morgan had been buying up shipping lines and combining them into a syndicate called the International Mercantile Marine Company and now the I.M.M. included a controlling interest in the Oceanic Steam and Navigation Company.

It was fear of an American takeover of the White Star Line by Morgan that prompted the British government to help Cunard raise enough money to build three more liners—the Aquitania, the Mauretania, and the Lusitania to compete with White Star.

In 1911, White Star launched the first of what would be a series of three sister ships, the Olympic, followed by the Titanic and the Britannic. The Britannic was originally scheduled to be called the Gigantic, but after the Titanic disaster it seemed more prudent to give her a less grandiose name.

By 1912, the year of the Titanic's maiden voyage, Ismay's son, J. Bruce Ismay, still held controlling interest of White Star and ran the London office.

The Britannic was launched three years after the Titanic sank. Unfortunately since the Britannic was launched during the outbreak of World War I, it never saw commercial service and became a hospital ship. In 1916, she was sank in the Adriatic after colliding with a mine. In a curious and ironic footnote, Violet Jessup, one of the nurses serving on board, had also been one of the survivors of the Titanic.

Until the Titanic's fatal maiden voyage, White Star symbolized elegance and opulence. Even after the Titanic, White Star's Olympic remained a favorite. By 1921, the company was bragging that the Olympic had carried more people across the ocean than any other vessel in the history of the world.

Until the 1930s, White Star ships were the epitome of elegance, despite the sinking of what had been called the line's most elegant and luxurious ship—the Titanic. Contrary to Titanic folklore, the White Star Line never boasted that their ships were "unsinkable." This hyperbole was promoted by the popular press, which wrote about the Titanic that "Not even God himself could sink this ship."

For the first quarter of the twentieth century, these two British lines, Cunard and White Star, battled with two German lines—North German Lloyd, which sailed from Bremen, and the Hamburg American Lines, which sailed from Hamburg—for supremacy of the Atlantic Ocean. In those early years, they competed more for steerage class passengers than for first-class passengers, since the growing immigration trade provided the bulk of their revenues.

Soon others entered the race for this growing passenger trade. In 1901 the Dollar Line was founded and in 1908, the Matson Line began service to Hawaii. In 1921, the United States Lines was founded. Soon the Italians, the Norwegians, the Swedes, and the Dutch followed suit and established their own passenger lines—the Italian Line, Norwegian American Line, Swedish

American Line, and the Holland America Line—all competing for the Atlantic trade.

Traditionally, White Star's ships all had names ending in "ic," and until the 1930s, and the launching of the two Queens—Mary and Elizabeth—all Cunard ships had names ending in "ia." The first three twentieth century liners—the Mauretania, the Lusitania, and the Aquitania—were named for ancient Roman provinces. Ironically the change in Cunard's naming tradition came about by accident in 1934. There had been a strong connection between Cunard and the English Royal Family since Cunard was made a baronet by Queen Victoria.

Cunard, the steamship company now merged with White Star in 1934, had decided on the name Queen Victoria for its newest ship, in keeping with its tradition of using names ending in "ia," until a misunderstanding ensued. The commonly accepted story is that when King George VI was informed that the new ship was to be named after England's most beloved queen, he replied that his wife, Mary, "would be overjoyed."

Another apocryphal footnote says that renaming the ship, the Queen Mary, may have saved Cunard face, but it cost thousands of dollars. According to one ship historian, Jane Hunter-Cox (whose husband owned Ocean Pictures, the on-board photographer service on Cunard ships since 1929) rumor had it that Cunard had warehouses full of paper and china with the name Queen Victoria on it. The entire lot was immediately destroyed.

British monarchs not only launched the Queen Mary, the Caronia, the first Elizabeth, and the Queen Elizabeth 2, but they were regular visitors aboard Cunard ships.

Photographs of the Queen, the Duke of Edinburgh, the Queen Mother, and the late Princess Diana hang on the walls of the QE2, outside the Queen's room. The Queen's colors hang in the room itself.

In the twentieth century, ships became national symbols of pride and many of the kings and queens of Europe presided over the launchings of their flagships. King Victor Immanuel helped launch the Italian Line's "Rex" and Queen Wilhelmina helped launch Holland-America's Nieuw Amsterdam.

The Post World War I era was the heyday for oceangoing travel. The 1930s, '40s, and '50s saw the emergence of the great passenger liners. It was during this period that the two Queens, the Mary and the first Elizabeth, the Normandie, the Rex, the Conte di Savoia, and the United States were launched.

In 1949, in what would be a prophetic move, the Cunarder Caronia, known affectionately as the Green Goddess because her hull was painted green, became a forerunner in the cruising trade.

The next crucial year would be 1958. It was not only the peak year for post-war oceanic travel, but the beginning of the end. In 1958 more than 1,036,000 passengers traveled on seventy different steamers. But on October 26, all that would come to an end. On that day, the first commercial passenger jet landed in Paris. This seven-hour flight would be a crucial turning point for ocean travel, more devastating than icebergs, hostile waves, or storms at sea. The jet would represent a challenge that the luxury liners could never overcome. From this period on, more and more people chose the faster route across the Atlantic. Soon the grand ladies of the sea would find their popularity diminishing as the younger generation opted for more speed and less luxury.

By the 1970s, there were fewer and fewer flags flying over New York City's harbor. Gradually, more and more of the flagships of the Cunard, Italian, Compagnie Generale Transatlantique, Swedish American, Norwegian American, United States, and the Zim Lines disappeared from the New York piers. Today there is only one ship that sails regularly to New York, the last Cunarder, the QE2.

Captain Ronald Warwick, master of QE2 and her dedicated historian reports that many ship historians erroneously report that QE2 was named after the first Queen Elizabeth. In fact that ship was named for the Queen Mother Elizabeth and the second Queen Elizabeth ocean liner was named for the present monarch, Elizabeth 2. That name created some controversy in Scotland, since the Scots never recognized the Tudor Elizabeth, Elizabeth 1, and thus to this day do not call the present queen, Elizabeth the second.

During the one-hundred-and-fiftieth anniversary celebration of Cunard in 1990, Warwick not only welcomed the Queen and Prince Philip on board QE2, but he made his own QE2 history by becoming the first captain in Cunard history to command the same ship as his father. Commodore William E. Warwick had been the first master of the QE2 and served until he retired in 1972.

Today economics have changed the entire ship industry. More and more passengers choose to "cruise" rather than "cross." The QE2 has had three major refits to keep her modern and adapt her to cruising.

Today while Cunarders such as the Vistafjord and the Royal Viking Sun cruise the world, the QE2 is the only ship that makes regular transatlantic crossings.

Due to space considerations, this book deals only with those ships that belong to the old "crossing" tradition and only those cruise ships that are part of this tradition will be included.

The Ships

The following is a history of the leading passenger ships of the world.

This is not intended to be a complete list of all passenger ships, but it will include most of the ships that we refer to in the text. The ships will be listed according to the shipping lines.

Since many of these ships were bought and sold many times, we have not included multiple names except for a few historically important exceptions. Many of these ships had extended lives with lesser known shipping lines and irrelevant usage for our story. So for those we have only included their launching dates. There may be a discrepancy in some of our dates of a year or so because some ship historians use the launching dates while others use the date of the maiden voyage.

Ships are prefixed by letters that designate their design or purpose: T.S.S.—Turbine Triple-screw Steamer, R.M.S.—Royal Mail Steamer, S.S.—Steam Ship, or M.S.—Motorship. We will not use these prefixes in listing the ships except where the initials are historically important.

Allan Line
    Corsican 1907–1915
    Grampian 1907–1925
    Hesperian 1907–1915
    Victorian 1904–1929
    Virginian 1904–1920
American Export Lines
    Atlantic 1982
    Constitution 1951–1997
    Independence 1951
    Savannah 1964. (The first and only commercial nuclear passenger ship, currently in mothballs.)
American President Lines (Formerly the Dollar Line)
    President Cleveland 1947
    President Coolidge 1938
    President Wilson 1948
    President Hoover 1957

President Jackson 1940
President Monroe 1940
President Polk 1940
President Wilson 1948
Anchor Line
Columbia 1906
Lancastria 1922
Tuscania 1922
T.S.S California 1923
The Bergen Line
Richard With 1995
Canadian Pacific
Empress of Britain 1906
Empress of Britain 1931
Empress of Britain 1956
Empress of Japan 1930–1966
Empress of Scotland 1942
The Collins Line
Arctic 1852
Atlantic 1856
Baltic 1857
Pacific 1857
The Cunard Steamship Company
Alaunia 1925
Albania 1911
Albania 1921
Andes 1852
Aquitania 1914–1949
Arabia 1852
Arcadia 1840
Asia 1850–1867
Aurania 1925–1957
Ascania 1911
Ascania 1925
Ausonia 1911
Berengaria (Launched as the Imperator in 1913 and given to Great Britain as war reparations in 1918. It was renamed and refitted in 1920 and served until 1938.)
Brittania 1840–1848. (Sunk as a target ship in 1880.)
Caldonia 1840
Campania 1893–1914
Carinthia 1925
Carinthia 1950s
Carmania 1893–1914
Carmania 1905–1931.
Carpathia 1903–1918. (The first ship to reach the Titanic survivors. She carried 705 of them to New York.)
Caronia 1905–1933
Caronia 1948–1967
Columbia 1840
China 1862–1879
Cunard Adventurer 1971
Cunard Countess 1976
Cunard Princess 1976
Etruria 1884
Europa 1848
Franconia 1911–1916
Ivernia 1900
Ivernia 1923
Ivernia 1950s
Laconia 1911
Laconia 1922
Lucania 1893–1909
Lusitania 1907 (In 1915 she was torpedoed by a German U-boat and sunk off Kinsale, Ireland.)

Mauretania 1907 (Scrapped in 1935)
Mauretania 1939–1965
Media 1947–1989
Niagara 1848
Oregon 1883 (Sunk in 1886)
Parthia 1947–1948
Pannonia 1903
Persia 1852
QE2 1967–present (Official maiden voyage in 1969)
Queen Elizabeth 1946–1968 (Burned in Hong King harbor in 1972, scrapped in 1974)
Queen Mary 1936–1967 (Currently a floating hotel in Long Beach, California)
Sagafjord 1983 (Bought from Norwegian American Lines)
Samaria 1922–1956
Saxonia 1900
Saxonia 1954
Scythia 1921–1958
Servia 1881–1901
Sea Goddess I and II 1986
Slavonia 1903 -1909
Sylvania 1957
Ultonia 1898–1917
Umbria 1884–1910
Vistafjord 1983 (Bought from Norwegian American Lines)
Dollar Line, founded in 1901
President Coolidge 1931
President Fillmore 1929
President Garfield
President Harrison
President Hoover 1931
President Hayes
President Johnson 1929
President Monroe
President van Buren
President Wilson
Furness-Bermuda Lines
Bermuda 1927
Fort Victoria 1920
Queen of Bermuda 1933
The French Line Compagnie Generale Transatlantique
Colombie 1931–1966
The France 1863
The France 1912 (Scrapped in 1935.)
De Grasse 1924 (Became the Empress of Australia in 1953.)
Flandre 1952
France 1961–1974 (Renamed and still in service as the Norway.)
Ile de France 1927–1959 (Rescued the survivors of the Andrea Doria in 1956.)
Lafayette 1930–1938
L'Atlantique 1931 (Burned at sea in the English Channel in 1933.)
La Bretagne 1888
La Champagne 1891
La Gastogne 1886
La Normandie 1885
La Provence 1906
La Touraine 1891
Liberte 1946–1962 (Originally launched as the Europa in 1929, but was given to France as war reparations for the loss of the Normandie.)
Normandie 1935 (Burned in 1942, scrapped 1946–1947.)
Paris 1921–1939
German-Atlantic Line

Hanseatic 1930
Hamburg 1926
Grace Lines
    Santa Rosa 1932
    Santa Paula 1932
    Santa Elena
    Santa Maria 1928
    Santa Rita 1932
    Santa Clara
    Santa Barbara
    Santa Inez
    Capac
    Condof
    Coya
    Cusco
    Charcas
    Chipana
    Curaca
Hamburg Atlantic Line
    Hanseatic 1930 (Former Empress of Japan)
Hamburg Amerika Line
    Albert Ballin 1923 (Renamed Hansa in 1935.)
    Amerika 1905
    Deutschland 1900
    Imperator 1913 (Became the Berengaria in 1920, scrapped in 1946.)
    Kaiserin Auguste Victoria 1906
    Vaterland 1914 (Became the Leviathan, scrapped in 1938.)
    Bismarck 1914–22 (Sold to White Star after World War 1 and became the Majestic Hansa in 1923.)
Holland America Line
    Maasdam 1952
    Nieuw Amsterdam 1938–1974
    Noordan 1984
    Rotterdam 1959–1997
    Statendam 1929
    Westerdam 1986 (Previously the Homeric)
    Ryndam/Waterman 1984
    Veedam 1929
    Volendam 1922–52
Home Lines
    Brasil 1945
    Doric 1973
    Homeric 1986
The Italian Line
    Andrea Doria 1952 (Sank in 1956 in a collision with the Stockholm.)
    Augustus 1928
    Augustus 1951
    Conte Biancamano 1925
    Conte di Savoia 1932 (The first ship to test the use of stabilizers, sunk in 1943)
    Conte Grande 1927–1961
    Cristoforo Colombo 1954–1983
    Guilio Cesare 1951–1973
    Flavia 1947–1989
    Raffaello 1965–1975 (Scrapped in 1983)
    Leonardo Da Vinci 1960
    Michelangelo 1965–1975 (Scrapped in 1983)
    Rex 1932 (Burned in 1944, scrapped 1947–1958)
    Saturnia 1925
    Vulcania 1926
Matson Line

    Lurline 1932
    Malolo 1927
    Manoa 1913
    Mariposa 1932
    Matsonia 1913
    Monterey 1932
Moore-McCormack Line
    Argentina 1938
    Argentina 1958
    Brasil 1938
    Brasil 1958
    Montara 1913
    Uruguay 1938
    Uruguay 1958
North German Lloyd
    Berlin 1909
    Berlin 1925
    Bremen 1858
    Bremen 1896–1929
    Bremen 1922
    Bremen 1929 (Destroyed by fire in 1941)
    Bremen 1959
    Columbus 1924
    Europa 1930 (Given to the French in 1946 as war reparations and renamed the Liberte)
    Kaiser Wilhelm der Grosse 1897–1914
    Kronprinz Wilhelm 1901
    Kaiser Wilhelm II 1903
    Kronprinzessin Cecilie 1907
    George Washington 1909 (Destroyed by fire in 1951)
    Homeric 1913 (Later bought by White Star)
    Stuttgart
Norwegian America Lines
    Stavangerfjord 1918–1964
    Oslofjord 1938
    Oslofjord II 1949
    Bergensfjord 1956
    Sagafjord 1965 (Sold to Cunard in 1983)
    Vistafjord 1973 (Sold to Cunard in 1983)
Peter Deilmann EuropAmerica Cruises
    Berlin 1990
    Deutschland 1998
    M.S. Dresden 1989
    Konigstein 1998
    M.S. Lili Marleen 1994
    M.S. Mozart 1989
    M.S. Princesse de Provence 1987
    M.S. Prussian Princess 1987
The Peninsula and Oriental Steam Navigation Company (P&0)
    Canberra 1961
    Oriana 1960
    Star Princess 1989
    Strathmore 1935
    Strathnaver 1931
    Viceroy of India 1929
Royal Viking Line (Now Cunard)
    Royal Viking Sea 1973
    Royal Viking Sky 1973
    Royal Viking Star 1972
    Royal Viking Sun 1988
    Royal Viking Queen 1987
Swedish American Line
    Drottningholm 1904–1946
    Gripsholm I 1925

Gripsholm II 1957
Kungsholm I 1928–1965
Kungsholm II 1953
Stockholm 1938
Stockholm 1941 (Collided with the Andrea
Doria in 1956)
Union Castle Line
Sterling Castle 1935
Transvaal Castle 1962
Windsor Castle 1960
Winchester Castle 1930
Warwick Castle 1930
Pendennis Castle 1958
Reina del Mar 1956 (Pacific Steam Navigation Company)
United American Lines
Reliance 1914 (Originally built by Hamburg-Amerika in 1913,
sold to United American Lines after the war)
Resolute 1914
Cleveland 1909
United States Lines
America 1940
Leviathan 1922
Manhattan 1932
George Washington 1933
Republic 1923 (Formerly the President Grant)
United States 1952 (Currently in Philadelphia harbor)
Ward Line
Morro Castle 1930–1934 (Burned off the New Jersey shore
on Sept. 8, 1934 and drifted ashore at Asbury Park, New
Jersey)
White Star Line
Adriatic 1872
Adriatric 1906
Atlantic 1871
Baltic 1871
Baltic 1903–1933
Britannic 1874
Britannic 1915 (Sank in 1916)
Britannic 1930–1961.
Celtic 1872
Celtic 1901
Cedric 1903
Cymric 1898
Georgic 1932
Germanic 1875
Homeric 1922 (Scrapped in 1936)
Majestic 1890
Majestic 1919–1939 (Formerly the Bismarck and the sister
ship of the Vaterland and the Imperator)
Olympic 1911–1937
Oceanic 1871
Oceanic 1899 (Scrapped in 1914)
Olympic 1911–1937
Republic 1872
Titanic 1912–1912
Teutonic 1888
Zim Line
Jerusalem 1953
Israel 1955
Shalom 1964
Zion 1957

Life at sea has changed since the days of Samuel Cunard. Today the only way that many can "cross" is vicariously by collecting bits and pieces of these great ships. These cherished mementos—the menus, china, and the gala ribbons saved by one generation—are now coveted and cherished by another generation.

Paintings, posters, postcards, and toy ships have always been popular collectibles. One of the most popular items for ship collectors has been the formal portraits of the ships taken on their maiden voyages. One of the most unique forms of this genre has been the large tin lithographic portraits of the ships that hung in the offices of shipping companies and travel agencies during the late nineteenth and twentieth centuries. In the age before mass communication, these images of the ships at sea intrigued and attracted passengers.

Today most of these sell for thousands of dollars, but there are other collectibles for people with smaller budgets or space constraints. Period postcards also evoke the feel and the romance of the sea, as do log cards, the cards given out on voyages showing the speed, time, and weather conditions of each voyage. Many of these early cards have wonderful portraits of the ships and fascinating photographs of their interiors and can be found for just a few dollars.

Models come in all sizes and price levels. Some collectors aim for those models that measure three to six feet in length and range in price from $500 up. Smaller models scaled in inches can sell for under $100. Cunard still sells models aboard their ships and prices range from $60 to $500.

Toy ships have fascinated children for hundreds of years, floating in ponds and bathtubs. Today these late nineteenth century toys, designed to be authentic copies of the great liners, are coveted by adults, many of whom played with them as children. Because of space constraints, we have had to limit our book and will not include these tin toy ships.

The following pages will attempt to show the mystique of those glorious days with a pictorial display of items relevant to this period. We have chosen what we think is a representative selection to show what ship life was like for those few privileged passengers who cruised and crossed on those "floating palaces of the sea."

Turn the page and begin.

A postcard of the M.S. Richard With. $2.

The supreme Cunard collectible, the Britannia silver cup given to Samuel Cunard by the citizens of Boston in 1840 after he established the first regularly scheduled transatlantic mail and passenger service from Liverpool to Boston. It is now on board QE2 on the upper deck in the Yacht Club Lobby.

In 1856 the Persia was described as one of the best steamers in the world. (See next page for reverse.)

Postcards of the Vistafjord, Royal Viking Sun, M.S. Dresden, and the QE2. $2 each.

A small metal model of Britannia made in England and sold on the QE2. $70.

This is one of a special limited edition of 2,000 Spode plates given out by Cunard in 1995 to its world cruise passengers. Other plates in the series were the Britannia, the Niagara, the Europa, and the Caldonia. $150 each.

The 1840 Caldonia was the Britannia's sister ship. $150.

The reverse of the plate.

The 1848 Niagara and Europa were troopships in the Crimean war. $150.

The reverse of the plate.

A large ironstone platter used on the Lucania in the 1890s. $375.

A souvenir spoon sold in the on-board gift shop of the Kaiserin Auguste Victoria. When the ship was built in 1906, Hamburg Amerika Lines intended to name her the Europa. Years later she was sold and became the Empress of Japan. $175.

A menu from Saturday, December 17, 1994 of a luncheon given aboard the QE2 in honor of the Duke of York. $5.

A souvenir spoon sold on the Amerika. When she was built in 1905 by Hamburg-America Line, she was called the largest liner afloat. In 1914 she was seized by the U.S. government and renamed the U.S.S. America and became a troop ship during the war. She resumed passenger service in 1921 as the U.S. Lines' America. $60.

A rare pre-World War I promotional booklet for the Hamburg American Line's Vaterland filled with photos of interiors. Later the Vaterland was seized by the U.S. government and became the Leviathan. $350.

Photos taken on board the Normandie. $30 each.

An album of photos taken on board the Normandie in November 1937 showing the crew, Captain Thoreux, and the public room interiors. $30 each picture, $1,000 for the book.

A rare pre-World War 1 promotional booklet for Hamburg American Line's Imperator filled with interior photos. The Imperator was later seized by England and given to Cunard and was known as the Berengaria. $300.

Two great liners—the Hapag Lloyd's Europa and Cunard's Vistafjord—share space at a Norwegian dock in 1996.

The Normandie sails into New York harbor past another grand lady of the sea, the Statue of Liberty.

A colored lithograph of Cunard's Umbria (40 x 26 inches), circa 1884, used as an advertisement for travel agencies. Notice that the Statue of Liberty is in the background on the right-hand side. $2,500.

Cunard's funnels are still painted Cunard red. White Star Line funnels were painted buff with black tops.

Cunard's Berengaria was formerly the North German Lloyd's Imperator. Notice that I. Bishop repainted her in 1924 in her new colors sailing into New York harbor past the Statue of Liberty (39 x 29 inches). Tin lithographs were frequently used by travel agencies to advertise the ship and are now prized collectibles ranging in price from $800 to $3,500. $2,500.

This colored offset lithograph on tin (39 x 29 inches) of the North German Lloyd Liner Imperator from a painting by noted New Haven artist I. Bishop in 1911. The large eagle on the bow was placed on the ship to increase her overall length. The eagle was lost during a North Atlantic storm in an early sea trial. These lithographs have more value when they are still in their original frame with the brass plaque inscribed with details on the line and the tonnage. $2,500.

A small postcard-size painting of Cunard's R.M.S. Saxonia. $50.

A lithograph on paper printed in England of the R.M.S. Mauretania (28.5 x 22 inches). The painting, by Frank Mason, is probably of the ship's maiden voyage. $100.

An "ivorex" plaque sold on the Queen Mary in 1936. $150.

A tin lithograph painting of the first France (38 x 25 inches), circa 1912. These dramatic depictions of ships at sea surrounded by tugs were popular promotion tools for early twentieth century travel agents. $1,800.

An anonymous offset colored lithograph on tin (38.5 x 25 inches) of a starboard view of the Cunard's Lusitania on her Liverpool to New York run. There are passengers on deck. The lithograph is enclosed by a faux rope frame. $1,500.

The Lusitania set sail from New York on May 1, 1915, with more than 2,000 people aboard. Just as she entered the Irish Sea on May 7, she was hit by a two torpedoes from a German submarine and went down off the Old Head of Kinsale. One hundred and twenty four Americans went down with the ship. Today many still believe that she was illegally carrying munitions to Great Britain. A similar faux rope framed lithograph on tin was also done of the Mauretania (not pictured, valued at $1,000).

A lithograph on paper (41.5 x 31 inches) of the Queen Mary and Queen Elizabeth. On July 25, 1947, the two queens passed each other in the Atlantic for the first time. Note that the Mary has three stacks and the Elizabeth, two. The original painting was probably done in the late 1940s or 1950s after the Elizabeth resumed commercial service. $75.

A 1930s promotional brochure showing the size and the capacity of the Queen Mary. $50.

A paper "take to pieces" model of the Queen Mary designed as a children's toy. The twelve decks are held together by two screws and, when taken apart, each deck shows a pictorial layout of the deck. In addition, when the three bottom decks are taken away, it is an accurate version of how the Mary sat at sea. This toy was manufactured by the Chad Valley Company in the late 1930s. With original box, $350.

Another children's paper toy model of the Queen Mary was a premium offer from Kellogg's Corn Flakes. Other liners in the series were the Normandie, the Bremen, and the Empress of Britain. The package states that "this model is made of specially treated paper to resist water. However, if the ship is allowed to stay in water too long, or if used in rough water that wets the superstructure, the model will sink." The package goes on to say that if dried properly, the model will float again. $300 each.

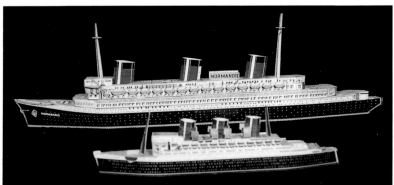

A colored print of the Normandie in a carved wooden frame (17 x 8 inches). $300.

A bronze model of the Normandie from 1935. $200.

A limited edition print (20 x 10 inches) of a formal portrait of the United States at sea. $250.

A small metal model of the United States, made in England. $100.

A letter card used on board the Queen Elizabeth. $10.

One of eleven aluminum sculptures that used to hang in the stairways of the S.S. United States. $5,000.

A lithograph on pressed board of the U.S. Lines' liner America sailing by the Statue of Liberty (29 x 20 inches). $100.

A hand-crafted wooden model of the America made by Lindsay in the United Kingdom in the 1950s. $200.

A plastic model of the United States, which lights up when plugged in. $500.

The handle from one of the two bridge doors on the S.S. United States. $5,000 per door.

A dramatic postcard of the Leonardo da Vinci with a picture of the famous Renaissance artist. $5.

A black and white postcard of the Aquitania. $5.

A reproduction postcard of a painting of the Britannia leaving Liverpool on her maiden voyage in July, 1840. Postcards are among the most popular ocean-liner collectibles. They are compact, inexpensive, and easy to store. $5.

A miniature hand-painted portrait on ivory sold on the Andrea Doria from 1953–1955. $1,000.

A lithograph on paper (26.5 x 19.5 inches) of the formal portrait of the France, signed Marin Marie. $100.

A reproduction postcard of the Persia one of the earliest Cunarders. $5.

A postcard of the 1900s Hamburg Amerika Prinzessin Victoria Luise on a cruise on the Norwegian coastline. $15.

A 1920s postcard of Anchor Line's California. $10.

A 1913 postcard of the Imperator with an inset showing off its eagle figurehead. $15.

A 1900s postcard of the Washington. $5.

In the 1900s, passengers often wrote about the weather. This is a series of twelve cards written each day on an October 11-19, 1897 voyage on the Bremen. The writer was often seasick. $150 for the set.

A 1910 postcard of the Lusitania. $10.

A 1920s postcard of the
Europa. $10.

A 1920s postcard of the
Bremen. $10.

On-board postcard of the
Vistafjord showing the
Cunard insignia, 1990s. $3.

Another postcard found on the
Vistafjord in 1996. $3.

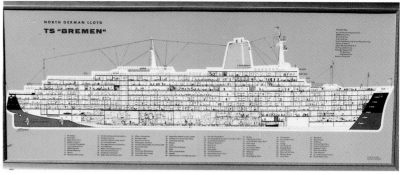

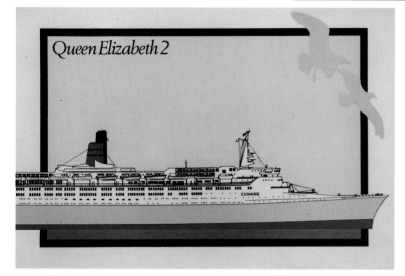

Top right:
A cross-sectional diagram of the 1959 Bremen showing all her cabin accommodations and public rooms (62 x 23 inches). $250.

Center right:
Lithograph on masonite of the Italian liner Rex (25 x 17.5 inches). $150.

Top left:
Two 1996 postcards of the Hapag Lloyd's Europa. $3 each.

Center left:
A 1980s stylized postcard of the Queen Elizabeth 2 in her post-Falklands War paint. $5.

Bottom right:
A travel agent's print of a photograph of the Leonardo da Vinci (14.5 x 22.5 inches). $150.

A mounted lithograph on masonite of the Gripsholm (28 x 17.5 inches). $75.

Left:
A framed menu from the last transatlantic ocean liner, the QE2, 1980s. (16.5 x 11.5 inches). $50.

A mounted lithograph of the Reliance (18 x 24 inches). $100.

A travel agent's print of the Liberte (27 x 20 inches) originally painted by Marin Marie. $250.

A travel agent's print of the Raffaello (21.5 x 10.5 inches). $150.

Chapter 2

Advertising and Promotional Materials

Posters, Calendars, Brochures, Log Cards, and Itineraries

In the late 1950s and '60s, Cunard advertised that "getting there was half the fun." But before the 1950s and the growth of the airline industry, ocean liners were not only the best way to get to Europe, they were the only way. New York piers were crowded with passengers booking passage, and ships sailed daily for years. Each line maintained a regular bi-weekly schedule of crossings.

On July 25, 1947, the two Queens passed each other for the first time in commercial service. From then on, one of the biggest thrills for Cunard passengers was that moment mid-ocean when the two Queens passed each other and gave a loud, long salute.

Until the late 1960s, size and speed were two of the most popular advertising tools for the shipping lines. And for years one of the biggest promotions was the race for the Blue Riband, the award given to the fastest ship at sea.

In the 1850s, Cunard steamships crossed the Atlantic in nine and a half days. But within a few years the German liners had broken this record and boasted that they were bigger, grander, and faster than any other ships at sea. It was at that point that the race for the Blue Riband soon became part of the excitement of an ocean crossing and captains began to compete with each other to set new records.

In 1897, the North German's superliner Kaiser Wilhelm der Grosse was launched as the world's largest liner. Within five months she had also earned the title of the fastest by taking the Blue Riband away from Cunard's Lucania. (We have spelled the Blue Riband with one "b." It is also spelled with two "b's," or as the English translation "Blue Ribbon.") The Kaiser Wilhelm der Grosse became the fastest ship crossing the ocean. Her record was five days and twenty hours in 1897. The next holder of this honor was the Deutschland.

In 1907, Cunard began an aggressive attempt to take control of the Atlantic run and launched what would become the first two in a long line of luxurious liners—the Lusitania and the Mauretania to compete wtih both the White Star Line and the North German Lloyd and Hamburg Amerika lines.

Until 1907, the German ships held the records for speed. In 1907, first the Lusitania, and then the Mauretania won the Blue Riband back from the Germans. The Mauretania's record speed was four days, ten hours, and fifty-one minutes. She held the record for the next twenty-two years, until it was taken from her by the Bremen. In 1927 she broke her own record by crossing in four days and nineteen hours. The next year the Germans regained the prize when the Bremen broke that record in August and crossed in four days and seventeen hours. Five years later the Italian liner the Rex made it across in four days and thirteen hours.

The Normandie claimed the record on her maiden voyage in 1935. Between the years 1936 and 1938, the honors went back and forth between the Queen Mary and the Normandie. In 1938, the Mary took the Blue Riband back and held it for the next two decades until 1952, when the United States scored a historic first and became the fastest ship in the world. The United States became the first American ship since the days of the Collins Line to regain the Blue Riband. She crossed in three days and ten hours. The race was over.

Ironically, until the 1990s, the crossing time remained constant at five days at sea. But in 1997, in order to save fuel costs, the QE2 announced that its transatlantic crossings would take six days and follow the less turbulent southern route across the Atlantic..

Speed wasn't the only selling point. Luxury and size were also big promotion tools.

In 1870, the French Line introduced running water on its ships. The Umbria and the Etruria were the first Cunarders to have electric lighting on board.

By the 1890s ships began to vie with each other to be the most luxurious and most opulent.

Company advertising brochures boasted that their ships had garden rooms, palm courts decorated with live plants, and public rooms decorated with antiques in the Chippendale, Sheraton, and Adam styles. The early German liners had marble bathrooms. In fact, marble bathrooms helped make the Imperator so top heavy that it tended to list.

In 1893, Cunard's Lucania became the first ship to have electric lights in the cabins, revolving chairs in the restaurant, and public rooms decorated with Persian tiles. The 1893 Campania was replete with stained-glass windows and mahogany and sandalwood panels carved by more than three-hundred Arab craftsmen. The library of the Mauretania was based on Louis XVI style. It also had a verandah cafe where it served food a la carte.

For years, the Olympic was considered the most popular ship afloat. Her main foyer rose four decks. Her on-board chapel was imitation Gothic. Her first-class lounge was modeled after the palace at Versailles. In addition, she boasted that she was the first liner to have a swimming pool and a full-size squash court on board.

Oceangoing passengers have always been concerned with maintaining their health and fitness at sea. As early as the 1900s, the Olympic had a fully equipped gymnasium with full-time instructors, "electric horses," bicycles, and rowing machines.

The Aquitania's grand lounge was decorated in the Palladium style, and the heavy paneling in her grill room was copied from paneling at the Royal Naval College in Greenwich.

Soon the ships reflected the best of their nation's culture. The Cunard/White Star ships served English savories and tea brewed the English way, and its public rooms had the ambiance of an English country home.

Hamburg/Amerika showed their ships were run with Prussian efficiency. They served German national dishes and beer in steins. Holland America kept its ships in bloom with flowers from Holland and decorated heavily with Delft tiles. The 1912 French Line flagship, the first France, was touted as the chateau of the Atlantic: "Versailles gone to sea." The Italian liner the Conte di Savoia was a seagoing replica of an Italian palazzo and the Ile de France was touted as the ultimate in seagoing Art Deco design, complete with the only at-sea merry-go-round.

By 1935, the Normandie outshone them all. She had a winter garden with tropical plants and foliage, caged birds, fountains, and lounge chairs upholstered in pinks, reds, and orange Aubusson tapestries. There were two sun-deck apartments with private terraces, four bedrooms, a living room, servant quarters, and a small private dining room.

The Nieuw Amsterdam's decorations included Venetian glass and Moroccan leather ceilings.

Size was another selling point. A 1914 company promotion for the Vaterland showed that the ship was so big that if she was upended it would top the Chrysler Building, then the tallest building in New York. White Star boasted that the Titanic was as long as a city block and, if upended, she would be taller than New York City's Singer Building.

In a 1937 Cunard/White Star picture book showing the Queen Mary's size, it was shown that the Queen Mary's main foyer and dining room were so spacious that they could hold the old Britannia and Columbus's three ships—the Nina, the Pinta, and the Santa Maria. Her refrigeration plant totaled 560,000 cubic feet and could meet the refrigeration needs of fifteen-thousand homes. Its three-acres of deck space were equivalent to the area of the Yale Bowl in New Haven, Connecticut; and her length equaled four New York City blocks.

The 1952 United States was advertised as fireproof and boasted that the only wood aboard was the grand piano and the butcher block. Everything else was aluminum and stainless steel. There is an apocryphal story that the United States' designer, William Gibbs, asked Steinway to build an aluminum piano. Steinway refused.

The United States represented a new era in ship design. Her designers made no attempt to conceal that she was a ship and not a floating hotel. In fact she was so sleek and shipshape that her critics said she resembled a troopship masquerading as a passenger ship. She was the first liner to be fully air-conditioned and was designed to be converted into a troopship with a capacity for a full division of sixteen-thousand troops within forty-eight hours. Additionally she had the capacity to sail round-trip, trans-Pacific without refueling and was rumored to be able to sail in excess of forty knots.

In 1982 it took eight days to convert the QE2 into a troopship carrying three-thousand men for service in the Falklands. In 1987 the QE2 became the last ship to use steam engines when she was taken out of service to be converted to electric diesel.

Some of the most interesting advertising collectibles are the itineraries, sailing schedules, log cards, posters, tin lithographs, mechanical calendars, ship models, and ship pins.

Advertising brochures are not only affordable, but offer fascinating insights into the lifestyles and destination choices of the times. Pre-World War II, there was a lot of nationalistic pride and the shipping lines were quick to capitalize on this.

Craftsmanship and style also categorize many of these collectibles. Beginning with the Ile de France, the Italian liners, and the Queen Mary, and culminating in the Normandie, ships of the 1930s developed a unique seagoing Art Deco style that was sleek, modern, and sophisticated. Gone were the pseudo-period pomp and fussiness that carried over from the Victorian age. The new ship chic was translated into the many posters of the era of which the French graphic artist A. M. Cassandre's 1935 poster of the Normandie remains the epitome of grand style.

We have not valued posters since the prices fluctuate. We have seen them sell for hundreds at flea markets and stores, at auctions for thousands. Lithographs of posters sell for $100 and up. Red Star Line poster advertising service from Antwerpen to New York and Philadelphia, late 1800s.

An American Line poster advertising service from Southampton direct to New York, 1900s.

A 1922 United States Lines' poster advertising the S.S. Leviathan as the largest ship in the world.

A 1920s White Star Line poster advertising that the Majestic is the world's largest liner, traveling from Southampton and Cherbourg to New York.

One of the most famous liner posters is Cassandre's 1935 poster of the Normandie. Copies sell for around $500. The original sells for $8,000-10,000.

A traditional style poster advertising the Normandie's express luxury service, 1935.

A 1910 White Star sailing schedule announcing future sailings of their new ship, the Titanic. $35.

A White Star announcement of the building of the Titanic, the largest steamer in the world. $35.

A plastic giveaway card calendar from the Cunard/Anchor Lines. $40.

The cover of an advertising brochure for the Lusitania-Mauretania. This was a 16-page brochure with photos and text, 3 x 8 inches, published by Cunard in 1907-1915. $100.

Inside page of the brochure announcing that the Lusitania and the Mauretania had attained "Safety, comfort, speed, luxurious fittings, and unsurpassed cuisine." $50.

A 1950s Cunard advertisement promising that "getting there is half the fun" when traveling on the Queen Elizabeth, Queen Mary, Caronia, Media, Parthia, Carinthia, Ivernia, Saxonia, or Sylvania. $10.

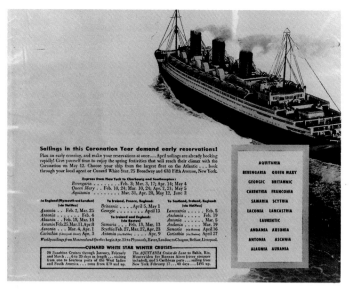

A 1937 Cunard advertisement for travel during "the Coronation year." This was for the coronation of Queen Elizabeth's father, King George VI, who became king after the 1936 abdication of his brother, the Duke of Windsor. In that year there were eighteen ships in the Cunard fleet and the Berengaria, the Aquitania, and the Queen Mary ran regular express service to New York and Cherbourg from Southampton. $15.

A photograph of a Cunard's Eagle Airways plane. $5.

A 1984 advertisement for a combination QE2 and Concorde trip. The first Cunarder to do a world cruise was the Laconia on a special charter in the year 1922-1923. In the 1950s Cunard began to investigate the possibility of creating an air-sea package to transport passengers to and from world cruise destinations. The Caronia was the first ship built to cruise as well as cross. In 1959 Cunard formed Cunard Eagle Airways, but by 1965, with the sale of the Mauretania and the decline in passengers, it had become unprofitable and Cunard sold it to British Airways. In the 1970s, Cunard and British Air promoted a more affordable land-sea package. The year 1984 was the only time that Cunard offered the Concorde at no extra charge to its first class transatlantic passengers. $5.

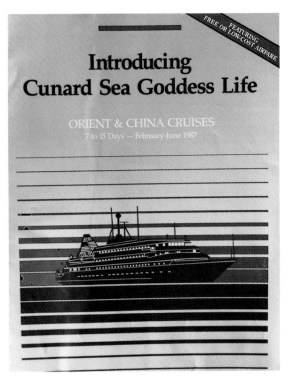

A 1987 promotional brochure introducing the Sea Goddess I. $5.

A 1935 magazine advertisement for Grace Lines to Peru and Chile. $5.

An advertisement for the American President Lines' S.S. President Cleveland and S.S. President Wilson, which sailed every three weeks from San Francisco and Los Angeles to Honolulu, Yokohama, Manila, Hong Kong, and Kobe. $5.

A 1940s Grace Lines magazine advertisement for cruises from New York to California. $5.

An Italian Line magazine advertisement. "The Lido deck is an Italian Line creation" claims this ad, which shows elegantly dressed passengers at night under a starlit sky. The Lido was an Italian word for beach and referred to the popular Lido beach and resort area in Venice. $5.

A French Line advertisement. "Wrap up in a sea breeze and relax." $5.

"People are moving back to Paris . . . This is the time when Bar Harbor, Newport, and Long Island Hamptons yield to autumn, to a gay house party in Scotland, to a partridge shoot at Rambouillet, or a sunny fortnight of golf at St. Jean -de-Luz." $5.

A 1947 Matson Line advertisement. "Matson knows the Pacific." $5.

A Hamburg American Line baggage tag from Hoboken to London and a Hamburg American Line passenger list. $35.

United States Lines' advertisement for the Panama Pacific Line. Photographs illustrate shipboard life, 1950s. $10.

A 1938 schedule of the Hamburg American Line and North German Lloyd's S.S. Columbus's cruise to South America. The following year the ship was scuttled by its crew to avoid capture by a British warship. $35.

A magazine illustration of the Leviathan stating that "ships of the United States Lines are the natural preference of American travelers. This Line provides the comforts and service that Americans enjoy and demand. While at sea you live amid all the luxurious and distinctly American features of your club or hotel." $10.

A 1950s full-size poster promoting service on the S.S. United States from Europe to America.

A 1920 publicity blotter for the White Star S.S. Homeric. $30.

A 1902 Cunard Line calendar advertising its Royal Mail steamers. Sailing days are marked in blue. $200.

A travel agents' display stand featuring the funnels of the Italian Line's Michelangelo/Raffaello. $100.

"Travel Will be Fun Again" promises this Canadian-Pacific Line advertisement for service from Shanghai to Southampton. $5.

A Compagnie Generale Transatlantique reverse glass mechanical calendar, circa 1952, with stylized portrait views of various French ocean liners, sea serpents, mythological figures, and mermaids painted on a celadon green wooden case. $350.

A reverse glass mechanical calendar for the Compagnie de Navigation Paquet Line for its Marseille, Paris, Casablanca, and Dakar run. $200.

A rectangular North German Lloyd reverse glass barometer showing a port view of the Europa against a gold leaf background, with a barometer in the center. $250.

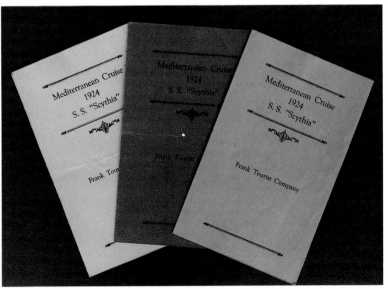

Mediterranean excursion schedules for the S.S. Scythia in 1924. $50.

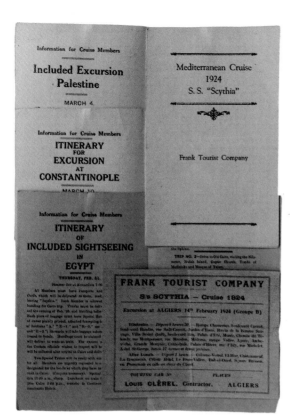

Excursion brochures for a 1924 Mediterranean cruise on the S.S. Scythia. $50 for the set.

Posters were created in eye appealing designs to set the mood of the sea and the elegance of the ship. This poster of the Aquitania in New York harbor was done by Kenneth Shoesmith in the 1920s and has sold for more than one thousand dollars.

An 1890s poster promoting third-class travel aboard the Lucania, Campania, Etruria, and Umbria. Travel time was five days, seven hours, and twenty-three minutes across the Atlantic; eight and five hours to Scandinavia. Other advertised amenities included a piano for the exclusive use of third-class passengers, third-class room berths fitted with wire-spring bottoms, and eating and drinking utensils cleaned by the company's stewards.

A 1930s Cunard poster for the Mauretania, Aquitania, and Berengaria.

Cunard's Europe-America
poster, 1920s.

A more traditional Queen Elizabeth poster, 1950s.

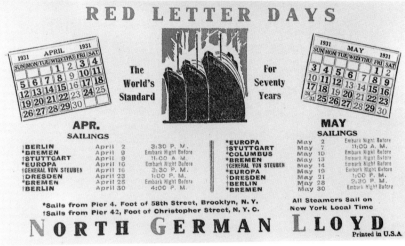

A 1931 advertising
card for North
German Lloyd
Line's ships the
Bremen, Berlin,
Stuttgart, Europa,
Dresden, and Gen-
eral Von Steuben.
$35.

A 1913 poster of a cut-away section of the
Aquitania. A copy hangs on the QE2 on the
Upper Deck E Stairway. $1,500.

A poster of the Caronia/
Carmania, 1920s.

A poster for the Berengaria, 1930s.

A French Line poster for the first France, 1900s.

A Holland America Line poster for the Potsdam.

A poster of the three North German Lloyd ships, the Columbus, Europa, and Bremen, 1930s.

A Holland America Line poster.

45

Chapter 3

Bon Voyage—Sailing Away

Tickets, Passenger Lists, Baggage Tags, Steamer Trunks, Cabin Keys

When British actress Beatrice Lillie first saw the Queen Mary she quipped, "Say, when does this place get to New York?" Rudyard Kipling called the Mauretania "the monstrous nine-decked city."

It is hard to describe the excitement of that first step up the gangplank and that first step aboard. Nothing prepares the first-time passenger for the luxury and size of an ocean liner or the suspense of opening the door of your cabin and settling into what will be home for the next few days, weeks, or maybe months. Some passengers get so attached to certain cabins that they will reserve them again and again.

In the heyday of ocean-liner travel, sail-aways were wonderful celebrations. In those pre-security-conscious days, friends would come aboard for a farewell bon-voyage party. The corridors would be filled with the sounds of popping champagne corks and festive partygoers. Cabins would be filled with bouquets of flowers. Ships would often depart at night, accompanied by a flurry of banners, balloons, and ribbons streaming down the ship. That final "last call for visitors" had much more meaning than it does today. Now few departing passengers are able to enjoy any hoopla with friends and must take solace in a solitary sip of champagne in their own cabin or enjoy a festive on-deck departure, looking around at faces, wondering who will soon become new shipboard friends.

Beginning in the 1920s, one of the must rituals was the sail-away photograph at a ship life ring, and once underway, the obligatory shot against the New York City skyline.

Today's embarkations are mostly anticlimactic, even though the QE2 still has uniformed personnel serving champagne to arriving passengers and there is still an eager shipboard photographer ready to snap that the sail-away pose.

The Peter Deilmann EuropAmerica Cruises has a simple gangway and a full tea service awaiting new passengers. Vistafjord and Royal Viking Sun serve champagne on deck.

But once underway, the sail-away is still romantic. Nobody is immune to the excitement of a New York departure and that moment of passage under the Verazzano Bridge or that last glimpse of the Statue of Liberty.

Nor does even the most jaded traveler tire of the glow of so many other legendary ports. I remember one sail-away aboard Royal Viking Sun as the ship sailed out of Venice. As we left this city of ducal splendor, a glass of champagne in hand sipping a silent toast, we saw on-shore cameras aim at the ship, flash and explode like fireflies in a summer night, and our ship, its decks now strung with necklaces of glittering lights, added to the wonder of a Venetian night.

On another sail-away off the island of Rhodes, we imagined the presence of the ghost of the giant Colossus looking down on us as the ship slowly pulled away from the harbor. That same night, the once grand Norwegian flagship, the Sagafjord, now overhauled and converted to a charter ship for the German travel market, sailed by and passed her former sister ship, the Vistafjord.

As the still-glorious cruiser passed the other, now a workhorse of the industry, in the starlit night, they saluted each other. Never have I heard a more mournful sound as the evening grew silent, filled with memories of grander days.

On QE2's first return to New York in 1990, after an unchartered rock off the coast of Martha's Vineyard put her in dry dock, she was greeted by an armada of New York City fireboats spouting celebratory sprays of water, circling press helicopters overhead, and an atmosphere of old-time nostalgia.

The 1997 departure of the Royal Viking Sun from Columbo, Sri Lanka, was marked by a musical salute by a troupe of classically dressed Sinhalese musicians and dancers from the old provincial capital of Kandy and, as the ship pulled out of the harbor, the drumbeats faded into the distance.

For the first half of the twentieth century, most of the English upper classes and many of the New York socialites who regularly crossed the ocean, traveled with their own help.

A 1902 Celtic passenger list listed passengers by name, adding "accompanied by maid or man-servant." Children traveled with their parents but were not entitled to a seat in the dining "saloon" unless full fare was paid.

But with the growing post-war democratization, fewer and fewer first-class passengers traveled with their own servants. The ships themselves provided personal valets to penthouse and sun-deck passengers; nannies and nurseries for those traveling with children; and dog pounds for cosmopolitan pets complete with the services of on-board walkers.

The France boasted that she not only had kennels on the sun deck, but that she provided special pet menus and her "dog walkways included a New York City hydrant and a Paris milestone."

Elizabeth Taylor, who routinely crossed on the Queen Mary, traveled with her dogs and would frequently ask the fish chef to provide special recipes for her pets.

The two Queens also had a complete staff of young bellboys who would run errands for first-class passengers.

Today, not only are maids a thing of the past, but the old-style valet has mostly disappeared. While most passengers send out clothes to the ship's laundry to be dry- cleaned, it is no longer an uncommon sight to see passengers, even those in first-class, doing their own personal laundry and ironing their own shirts and clothes in the on-board laundry room. Most ships provide washing machines and clothes-dryer facilities.

While the QE2 is slowly evolving with the times, it remains the last bastion of the British tradition of service. Many of the crew have served Cunard ships for years.

For years one of the most senior members of the crew of QE2 was the gentleman's valet, Geoffrey Coughfrey. Coughfrey, who went to sea the first time in 1948 on the Aquitania as a tourist-class waiter, prided himself on representing the best of the old Cunard tradition. When he retired he was the head valet of the Penthouse deck of QE2 and had served not only royals such as the Duke and Duchess of Windsor, the Queen Mother, and Princess Diana, but such theatrical luminaries as Vivien Leigh and Elizabeth Taylor. In those days his chores included unpacking and packing their suitcases, pulling back the curtains in the morning when he brought in their breakfast trays, serving tea in the afternoons, and bringing in cocktails as they dressed for dinner.

Coughfrey recalled that in the early days, everyone traveled with a maid or a nanny for the children. Today the old maids' rooms on QE2 have been converted into linen closets.

Coughfrey served morning toast with damson plum preserves and evening martinis to European society members and American millionaires . His lifetime motto of service was "never argue, just carry out their requests and smooth things out."

Former QE2 captain Commodore John Burton-Hall, observed his own tradition. He never sailed over the resting place of the Titanic, an area he referred to as a cemetery. Like most modern captains, Burton-Hall invited passengers to his cabins for cocktails and to his table in the Caronia dining room, gave daily talks on the ship, and hosted gala cocktail parties.

When longtime QE2 social director Maureen Ryan first went to sea in 1961, she was a telephone operator aboard the Queen Mary and one of a small handful of women. Today one third of the QE2 crew is female.

Ryan said that, in the 1960s, shipboard social life and the entertainment schedule relied heavily on the passengers themselves. Today most entertainment comes from a large troupe of professional singers, dancers, comedians, musicians, magicians, and a full-time cruise director's staff.

A new Cunard tradition is the "gentleman escort." Since women passengers outnumber men aboard, the line hires ten or twelve "gentlemen escorts" for each crossing to dance and mingle with unescorted ladies.

Children have always traveled with their parents, but today ships have better equipped playrooms. On a 1970s crossing on the France, there were so many young children that the ship had a full schedule of children's activities and a full staff of attendants who organized events from early in the day through the evening.

On a recent trip on the Bergen Line's M.S. Richard With, which sails the remote mail-boat route along the coast of Norway, there was a separate playroom area for children filled with play equipment and climbing toys.

Before the 1970s, oceangoing ships practiced a strict segregation of classes. It was almost impossible to cross the barriers. A 1960s passenger recalls a trick he learned while traveling as a young college student. To get into the public rooms of another class, he followed the lifeboat arrows in reverse.

I can remember being stymied in the halls of QE2 and on the France as I tried to maneuver the barriers between first and second class and descend to the more lively dance floors and bars of second class.

Today, all that is left of the old stratification is a puzzling arrangement where up and down stairways often end suddenly, and passengers must return to the mid-ship stairways to achieve access to those parts of the ship formerly reserved to an old class system. "Just remember the "E" stairway is for everything," said one veteran ocean traveler.

In the early days of the twentieth century, Cunard and White Star would charge as much as 200 pounds sterling for a week's crossing in first class. At the same time, steerage passengers were paying as little as 20 pounds.

Today economics and the growing informality of twentieth century life have made a visible change in both shipboard life and shipboard dress. And the tuxedo and evening dress, the last visible bastions of privilege, are becoming increasingly rare sights.

Beginning in the 1970s, the traditional upper-class custom of dressing for dinner began to be assailed by the more casual lifestyles of American society. Today, jackets and ties are still required in Cunard's grill rooms, on gala nights, and at captain's dinners, and most passengers still dress formally on nights when the ship is at sea. But the new rule is that on sailaway nights and on the last night aboard, informal and often casual travel clothes are allowed in all dining rooms. The rationale is that since people no longer travel with help to do the packing and unpacking, concessions must be made.

One of the ironies of this new democracy is that often many who can afford the upper-priced rooms prefer to pay less and dine informally. And ships responding to this need have created a growing number of restaurant buffets where formal attire is not required.

Among the most fun collectibles are the ship passenger lists, the stylish baggage tags, the cabin keys, and the other mementos of the sail-away. There is an untapped treasure-trove of paper memorabilia (ephemera) such as old tickets, baggage slips, and used baggage tags yet to be retrieved from old albums lying on shelves in dusty book stores and flea markets. Old keys are prized by key collectors as well as ocean liner buffs.

While Louis Vuitton has always been the ultimate in luggage collectibles and his trunks were often found among the chic first class passengers, the older steamer trunks, complete with labels, drawers, and hangers, can still be found in corners of junk shops, at garage sales, or scattered among flea market offerings.

We found our steamer trunk lying on the ground near the garage of a house in New Hartford, Connecticut. We bought it for $50 from a couple glad to get it out of their home. We later learned that it had been owned by a Hartford, Connecticut, insurance executive who had traveled aboard many Cunard/White Star ships such as the Queen Mary, Hamburg American lines, North German Lloyd, and Swedish American ships. If only those old baggage labels pasted to its sides could talk!

Bon Voyage. The authors leave from New York on the thousandth voyage of the QE2, June 14-19, 1995.

A 1910 second cabin passage ticket for the Lusitania. $20.

Two early 1900s plastic baggage tags with leather straps for the Cunard and the Cunard-Anchor Line. These tags were used as both luggage and cabin keys. $45 each.

A Cunard White Star baggage label for the Queen Elizabeth. Luggage could be marked "wanted" for the cabin or "unwanted" to be stored until arrival on land. $15.

A 1990s first-class QE2 luggage tag. $5.

Another Cunard/White Star stateroom baggage label. $10.

A 1935–1939 metal medallion attached to cars being shipped on the Normandie. $300.

A 1980s QE2 luggage tag. $10.

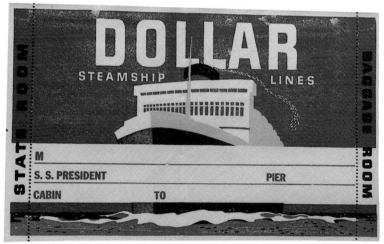

A Dollar Line's pre-World War II bag label used on one of its ships. All Dollar Line ships were named for U.S. presidents. $15.

A French Line baggage room tag. $15.

An Ile de France luggage label. $15.

A baggage tag from the France. $15.

A Flandre luggage label. $15.

A first-class baggage tag from the France. $15.

A France tourist-class baggage tag. $15.

A North German Lloyd stateroom baggage tag in German. $15.

A North German Lloyd stateroom baggage label in English. $15

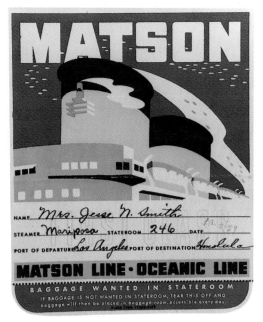

A 1929 Matson Line baggage label for the steamship Mariposa. $10.

A 1996 Europa baggage label. $5.

A 1995 Peter Deilmann EuropAmerica baggage label and baggage tag for the Princesse de Provence. $5.

A Holland-America cabin class baggage label. $10.

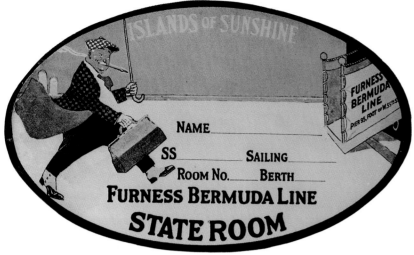

A 1930s Furness Bermuda Line's stateroom label. $25.

A 1930s plastic Italian luggage tag for the Conte Grande. $45.

A 1950s first-class United States luggage tag. $15.

Colored luggage tags used in 1997 for disembarkation on the Royal Viking Sun. $3 each.

A plastic luggage tag for the Andrea Doria. $75.

A Cunard QE2 ticket with leather ticket case. $10.

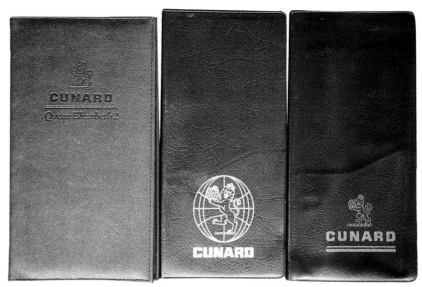

Three versions of Cunard ticket holders from the 1980s through the 1990s. $10 each.

A money pouch for a passenger on the Bremen, circa 1900s. $50.

The other side of the money pouch showing a portrait of the ship.

A metal and enamel sign from the 1920s used on Cunard ships. $225.

Cunard credit cards, 1990s. Most passengers charge all bar bills, laundry, etc. to their credit card and pay their final account when they leave. Frequently on the morning of embarkation, the purser will broadcast the names of passengers with delinquent accounts. $5 each.

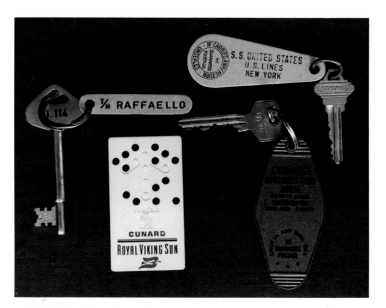

A 1996 key from QE2, $15; a 1996 key from the Royal Viking Sun, $5; a 1950s key from the United States, $60, and a 1970s key from the Raffaello, $40.

Ship cabin keys from the Rodam, $25; the S.S. Monterey, $20; QE2, $25, and the Andrea Doria, $60. Cabin keys can range in price from $15 to $60.

A key from the United States Lines' S.S. Washington. $60.

A June 15, 1895 passenger list for the American Lines' S.S. Kensington. $35.

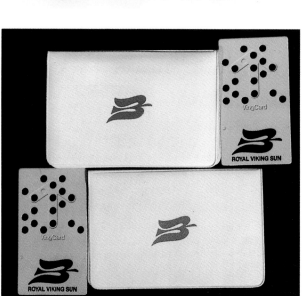

Two 1997 new "hotel style" keys from Royal Viking Sun with their plastic key cases. $5.

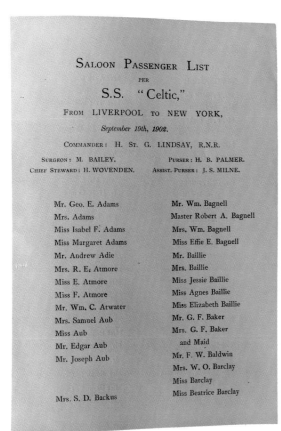

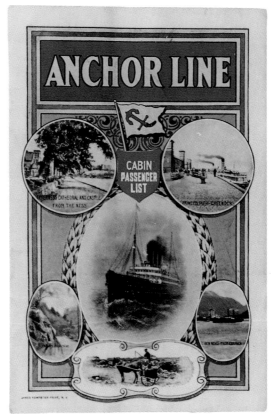

A 1906 Anchor Line Cabin passenger list for the S.S. Columbia's crossing from New York to Glasgow. $35.

A 1902 saloon passenger list on the White Star's S.S. Celtic. Notice that Mrs. G. F. Baker traveled with her maid. $35.

A September 1902 Saloon passenger list for the White Star's Celtic. $35.

A beautiful cover on the September 1921 list of first-class passengers on the S.S. Canopic. On the inside page there's a gorgeous picture of the Olympic. $25.

A White Star Line sailing schedule. $35.

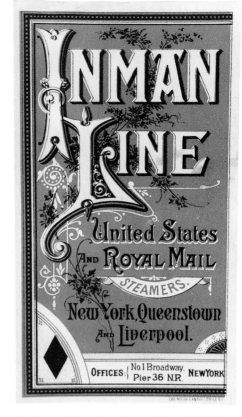

An Inman Line brochure of Royal Mail Steamers' service schedules to the United States. The Inman Line was one of many early transatlantic passenger lines owned by J.P. Morgan. $35.

A 1894 hand-colored passenger list for the Bremen. $35.

A 1927 Red Star passenger list for the return of the second A.E.F. (American Expeditionary Force) from Paris. Shown are the boxcars that held forty men or eight horses. $15.

A 1931 passenger list from the Stuttgart. $35.

A 1938 Grace Line passenger list from the Santa Rosa. $30.

A May 28, 1964 passenger list for a crossing from New York to Southampton for the United States, "the world's fastest and most modern liner." $35.

A 1905 visitor ticket admitting a Hamburg-American line passenger on the ship S.S. Patricia on the day it sailed. $15.

A 1997 passenger list for the "Jewels of the East" segment of the world cruise of the Royal Viking Sun. $5.

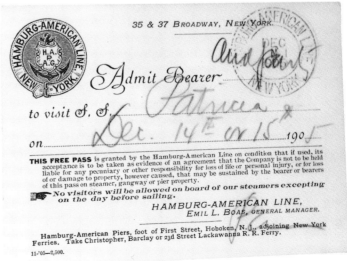

Log cards were given away as souvenirs showing each day's mileage and weather. This log card cover shows the Celtic at dock in Liverpool. $35.

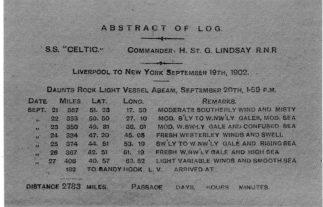

A 1902 log card for White Star's Celtic crossing from Liverpool to New York. $35.

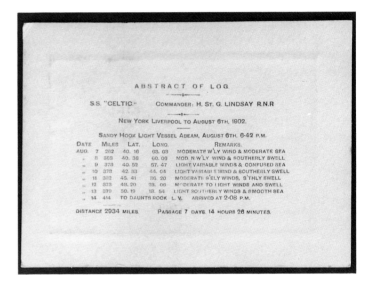

A 1902 log card from the S.S. Celtic's crossing from New York to Liverpool. The voyage took seven days, fourteen hours, and twenty-six minutes. $35.

The covers of two log cards from the Mauretania and the Carmania. $35.

Log cards showed the interiors of some of the great liners of the day such as this illustration of the library on the White Star's Oceanic. $35.

THE CUNARD LINE R.M.S. "CAMPANIA" AND "LUCANIA," 12,950 TONS.

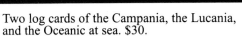

OCEANIC AT SEA

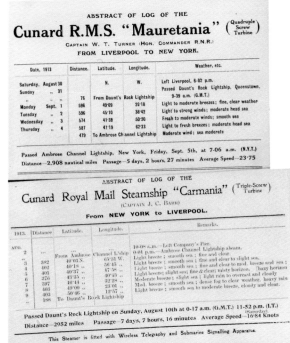

ABSTRACT OF LOG OF THE

Cunard R.M.S. "Mauretania" (Quadruple Screw Turbine)

CAPTAIN W. T. TURNER (Hon. Commander R.N.R.)

FROM LIVERPOOL TO NEW YORK.

Date, 1913	Distance	Latitude	Longitude	Weather, etc.
Saturday, August 30		N.	W.	Left Liverpool, 6·02 p.m.
Sunday, " 31	76	From Daunt's Rock Lightship		Passed Daunt's Rock Lightship, Queenstown, 9·39 a.m. (G.M.T.)
Monday, Sept. 1	596	49·09	25·18	Light to moderate breezes; fine, clear weather
Tuesday, " 2	596	45·10	38·42	Light to strong winds; moderate head sea
Wednesday, " 3	574	41·38	50·20	Fresh to moderate winds; smooth sea
Thursday, " 4	587	41·19	62·23	Light to fresh breezes; moderate head sea
	479	To Ambrose Channel Lightship		Moderate wind; sea moderate

Passed Ambrose Channel Lightship, New York, Friday, Sept. 5th, at 7·06 a.m. (N.Y.T.)
Distance—2,908 nautical miles Passage—5 days, 2 hours, 27 minutes Average Speed—23·75

ABSTRACT OF LOG OF THE

Cunard Royal Mail Steamship "Carmania" (Triple-Screw Turbine)

(CAPTAIN J. C. BARR)

From NEW YORK to LIVERPOOL.

1913.	Distance	Latitude	Longitude	Remarks
AUG.				10·08 a.m.—Left Company's Pier.
2	...	From Ambrose Channel L'ship	65·31 W.	0·01 p.m.—Ambrose Channel Lightship abeam.
		40·03 N.		Light breeze ; smooth sea ; fine and clear.
3	382	40·18 ..	56·45 ..	Light breeze ; smooth sea ; fine and clear to slight sea.
4	402	40·37 ..	47·58 ..	Light breeze ; smooth sea ; fine and clear to mod. breeze and sea ;
5	401	43·35 ..	40·43 ..	Light breeze; slight sea; fine & clear; misty horizon. "hazy horizon
6	376	46·44 ..	32·28 ..	Moderate breeze ; slight sea ; light rain to overcast and cloudy
7	397	49·00 ..	23·01 ..	Mod. breeze ; smooth sea ; dense fog to clear weather, heavy rain
8	403	50·46 ..	12·57 ..	Light breeze ; smooth sea to moderate breeze, cloudy and clear.
9	188	To Daunt's Rock Lightship		

Passed Daunt's Rock Lightship on Sunday, August 10th at 0·17 a.m. (G.M.T.) 11·52 p.m. (L.T.) (Saturday).
Distance—2952 miles Passage—7 days, 7 hours, 16 minutes Average Speed—16·84 Knots.

This Steamer is fitted with Wireless Telegraphy and Submarine Signalling Apparatus.

A 1913 log card for the Mauretania. She made the trip from Liverpool to New York in five days, two hours, and twenty-seven minutes. And a 1913 log card for the Carmania. She made the crossing from New York to Liverpool in seven days, seven hours, and sixteen minutes. $35 each.

Two log cards of the Campania, the Lucania, and the Oceanic at sea. $30.

ABSTRACT OF LOG OF THE

Cunard White Star R.M.S. Aquitania

CAPTAIN R. V. PEEL, R.D., Commodore R.N.R.

FROM SOUTHAMPTON TO NEW YORK via CHERBOURG.

Date, 1935	Distance	Latitude	Longitude	Weather, etc.
Wed'day, July 24		N.	W.	At 2.30 p.m. B.S.T. Left Coy's Pier, Southampton
" " 24				At 7.44 p.m. B.S.T. Arrived Cherbourg
" " 24				At 9.25 p.m. B.S.T. Left Cherbourg
Thursday, " 25	360	49·59	10·49	Moderate breeze, mod. sea, fine and clear
Friday, " 26	560	49·11	25·09	Moderate head breeze, mod. sea, cloudy and clear
Saturday, " 27	548	46·49	38·20	Fresh head wind, rough sea, cloudy and clear
Sunday, " 28	546	43·00 d.r.	50·00 d.r.	Fresh breeze, rough sea, overcast and clear
Monday, " 29	567	41·31 d.r.	62·56 d.r.	Fresh varying winds, rough sea, cloudy, clear
Tuesday, " 30	515	To Ambrose Channel L'ship		

Passed Ambrose Channel Lightship, New York, on Tuesday, July 30, at 11.00 a.m. (E.D.S.T.)
Distance—Cherbourg to Ambrose Channel Light Vessel 3,096 nautical miles
Passage—5 days, 18 hours, 35 minutes Average Speed 22.34 knots.

A 1935 log card from the Aquitania. She crossed from Southampton to New York with a brief stop at Cherbourg in five days, eighteen hours, and thirty-five minutes. Originally, Cunard ships sailed from Liverpool. By the 1930s they were sailing from Southampton. Until the 1990s, most Cunard crossings included a stop at Cherbourg. Today, Cunard stops in France infrequently. French liners sailed from Le Havre. The France's last eastbound crossing in September 1974 came to an abrupt end when the crew mutinied outside Le Havre and held the authorities at bay to protest the ship being removed from service. $35.

Passengers leave their passports with the ship's purser and receive in exchange a ship's landing card. A different color card is handed out at each port. The crew gets a separate landing card. These are from a world cruise on the Royal Viking Sun. $5 each for passenger cards; $15 for a crew member's card.

A log card with a color illustration of the Aquitania. $20.

R.M.S. "Aquitania" - Cunard Line

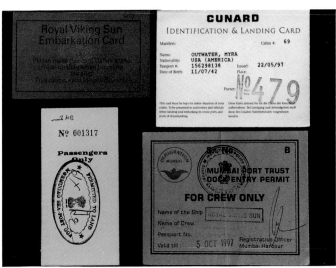

Chapter 4

Inside Your Cabin

Furnishings, Soaps, Towels, and Stationary

Life was different in the early days of commercial ocean voyages. Taking a ship was a means to an end, transportation from point A to point B. In fact, the word "liner" meant a ship that traveled in a line from one point to the next. It wasn't until the late 1890s that ships became floating worlds of luxury for first-class passengers and a means to a new life for the hundreds and thousands who traveled in steerage.

One of Samuel Cunard's most famous passengers was Charles Dickens, who crossed on the Britannia in 1842.

"I felt like a giraffe being persuaded into a flower pot," said Dickens describing his cabin aboard the Britannia. It's no wonder that Dickens added that he was also seriously seasick throughout the voyage.

Through the years seasickness has remained part of the ocean-going experience. One of the earliest remedies was Mother Sill's seasick pills. Ginger has also been a traditional stomach restorative for sailors and QE2 still offers trays of crystallized ginger outside her dining rooms. But even though the Queen Mary was known to have a 40-degree roll, few have ever regretted the few moments of discomfort.

In Dickens' day the only way to get across the ocean was by ship. It was a spartan life. State rooms were swept daily at five o'clock in the morning. Dickens described his accommodations as "an utterly impractical and thoroughly hopeless and a profoundly preposterous box. . . a bunk where beds were shelves covered with tiny mattresses and a limp quilt. Nothing smaller for sleeping in was ever made except coffins."

The earliest ships accommodated only cabin passengers. It would not be until the late nineteenth and early twentieth centuries that the great exodus of immigrants would crowd the lower decks of the ships, bringing in not only a large new source of revenue for the ocean liners, but an influx of future passengers who would grab hold of the proverbial gold ring and return years later to visit the homeland and the families they left behind.

Dickens' Britannia had space for one-hundred-and-fifteen persons. Today's ships can carry more than seventeen hundred passengers.

Pre-World War I ships were divided into first class, second class, and steerage. Until the 1920s when there were changes in U.S. Immigration Laws, immigrants in steerage provided a major source of income. By the 1930s the waves of immigration were slowed and shipping lines recognized that profitability depended on marketing their ships more for first- and second-class passengers.

In the 1930s, first-class would be called "cabin class," an often confusing category for ship historians, since later cabin class became a third-class designation. After the second World War, the designations once more were first-, second-, and third-class. For one brief moment, another classification, "tourist class," was added. This designation, which included third and the then cabin class, resulted in a lot of confusion. From the 1960s through the 1980s there were two classes aboard QE2, first and transatlantic class. Today, the only designation of class is the dining-room affiliation. On QE2, first-class passengers eat in the Grill Rooms—the Queen's, the Princess, and the Britannia Grill. On most cruises, people are categorized by their dinner seatings. Usually the occupants of the higher-priced cabins prefer to eat at the later seating.

Until Albert Ballin became the president of the Hamburg Amerika line, shipboard decor was not notable. Ballin became the first to hire land-side interior decorators and chefs de cuisine, and to imbue his ships with a hotel-like atmosphere.

While today most ship passengers assume that they will have all the comforts of land, including a television and a VCR inside their cabins, it wasn't until the end of the nineteenth century that cabins even had private bath facilities.

The Collins Line flagship, the Atlantic, advertised that she had individual bathrooms for first-class passengers and steam heat in some of the cabins. Most other ships only provided baths for the penthouse cabins and the rest of the passengers would have to register upon embarkation with a bath steward and book a daily twenty-minute bath time. White Star cabins had the most passenger amenities. Cabins had electric call bells, were double the size of other liners, and the dining saloons were large enough to fit all passengers in a single sitting. The Olympic was touted as the most luxurious super liner of its time, but even so, only a few cabins had plumbing or private bath facilities.

When the White Star's Olympic was launched in 1911, it advertised that outside cabins had baths, but there was no provision for baths for any of the inside cabins. By 1928, the line had made provisions for bathrooms for most of her inside cabins.

Up to the mid-1950s the Cunard ships still had only saltwater baths available. The Line provided a special saltwater soap that would produce a reasonable lather. The Queen Mary had faucet controls for both salt and fresh water.

The furniture in early transatlantic steamers in the late 1890s was usually bolted in place to the deck. Furnishings were usually designed to maintain balance and were amazingly stable. Beginning in the 1870s, individual iron swivel chairs were bolted to the deck. By 1910, the companies were beginning to install freestanding chairs.

The earliest cabins were sparsely furnished. Most cabins had an upper and lower bunk and a horsehair sofa that could double as a children's cot. Shipboard sofas were always fourteen inches above the ground so that a thirteen-inch-high trunk could be stored underneath.

Early passengers wore serviceable clothes such as heavy tweeds, homespun clothes, and, especially, no-nonsense shoes because the decks were often slippery and dangerous.

It wasn't until the late 1890s, when more and more passengers traveled with steamer trunks, that formal clothes became *de rïgueur* aboard ship. In fact, corridors on later ships would become wider and wider to allow the crew to carry these trunks down below.

Women have served aboard passenger ships since the mid-1800s as companions and stewardesses to unaccompanied ladies.

By the late 1890s and early 1900s, passengers began to travel with servants. And it was because of this on-board presence of help that the tradition of dressing for dinner at sea became possible. And the society women would change their costumes many times throughout the day.

Said Lady Cynthia Asquith, a survivor of the Titanic, "It must be admitted that a very large fraction of our time was spent dressing and undressing. We were forever changing our clothes, a custom that necessitated traveling with a mountain of luggage, at least one large domed trunk called a Noah's Ark, an immense hat box, and heavy fitted dressing case."

It might be added that help was such an important part of the life of the rich that one of the passengers on the Titanic was traveling with both his chauffeur and his newly acquired Renault touring car.

Wardrobe trunks were an essential part of the ocean-going travel experience. They were more like traveling closets/bureaus than the storage trunks used today. When opened, half of the trunk revealed hanging rods, the other half revealed drawers. The advantage was that they never needed to be packed or unpacked and could be just opened or closed.

Often travelers would travel with two sets of luggage, a trunk to be used on board and another trunk to be stored in the hold, to be available on arrival.

Today, cabins are still shipshape, but the newer ships are designed with larger more luxurious accommodations that look more like those found in a land resort. In the 1980s, the QE2 was redesigned to allow for more closet space in her cabins.

While most ships no longer store passengers' luggage for the duration of the voyage, most cabins have enough space for extra items. Some of the smaller ships, like those of the Deilmann line, have enough space under the bunks for extra luggage.

One of the most nerve-racking experiences once aboard is that first hour when the ship is underway and you must wait for your luggage to be delivered to your cabin. Despite the awesome mounds of bags, trunks, and hanging bags, most bags arrive miraculously in the cabins within the first hour or two of the voyage.

Today, on-board luxury liners gift shops stock so many clothes and outfits that it would be possible to buy almost all your traveling wardrobe, with the exception of underwear and shoes. Recently Cunard began offering its own line of cruise-wear clothing, from leisure wear to formal clothes.

Once underway, life at sea assumes its own rhythm and the ship creates its own time zone. Clocks eastbound are advanced an hour each day. Clocks on westbound crossings are turned back an hour each day. Once under way, days at sea blend into each other. The Royal Viking Sun helps its passengers keep track by changing the elevator mat to indicate the day of the week.

Life aboard has changed little since the early days of twentieth century ocean crossings. It is still luxurious and each night, a full schedule of the next day's events is slipped under the cabin door, and passengers can choose to mingle, get involved or just spend the days relaxing on deck.

Life still revolves around meal times, tea times, and cocktails. At the beginning of the century, meals would be announced by the sounding of a small Chinese gong. Today, mealtimes are announced on the speaker system. The day begins with an early coffee on deck in one of the public rooms for early risers. At 7:30 a.m., a large open buffet or a formal seated breakfast is served in the dining rooms. At mid-morning, bouillon is served on deck or, if the weather is inclement, in the lounge.

Luncheon is served at 1 p.m. in the dining room or buffets are served at 12:30 in the Lido. Afternoon tea begins with some ceremony at 4 p.m. and the cocktail hour begins shortly thereafter.

Dinner is either served in two seatings beginning at 6 p.m. or at one seating beginning at 7 p.m. At 11:30 p.m. a buffet is served in one of the dining rooms.

There is a huge variety of cabin mementos available on land for the sharp-eyed collector—lamps, telephones, vases, blankets, stationery, and desk accessories. Soaps and lotions are collectible because they show the changing logo styles employed aboard. Contemporary photographs of cabins are also fascinating. There are still many maiden voyage brochures available, as well as deck plans, passenger lists including the names of the rich and famous from the worlds of theater, politics, and the movies. Today anyone can travel. In those days, it was only the rich who could afford it. Today there are cruises to fit every budget, and every time frame. In those days only a very few had the time to leisurely cross the ocean.

In 1931, Oliver Herford made fun of some of the more tiresome aspects in his book *Sea Legs*:

"D's the Deck-steward
With careful financing
He will give you a chair
Where the view is entrancing.

E's the electrical Horse
In the Gym
It won't get you far
but 'twill keep you in trim."

"O is the Ocean
a watery waste
With a nauseous motion
and a terrible taste."

"T's Tipping, a ticklish
topic to touch;
The Rich tip too little
the Poor tip too much."

A 1900s stateroom. Illustration. $10.

Marlene Dietrich in her stateroom aboard the Normandie.

Great hordes of Eastern European immigrants came to America from the late 1890s through the early 1900s before stricter immigration laws were instituted in the 1920s. They not only brought their talents to America, but also provided much of the revenue of the early twentieth century passenger trade for the shipping lines. A postcard shows immigrants on deck. $2.

If only this steamer trunk could talk. It traveled extensively in the 1920s, 1930s, and the 1940s on ships such as the Bremen, the Queen Mary, and Swedish American ships. $75.

A 1950s first class accommodations list handed out to Queen Elizabeth passengers. $35.

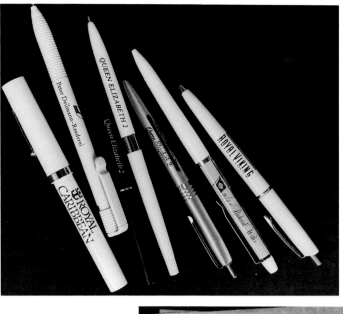

Ship pens used aboard in the 1990s. $5 each.

Cocktail napkins used aboard the Bergen Line's Richard With in 1997. $2.

Lifeboat drills are a common event aboard ships and are usually held the first day for passengers and during the voyage for the crew. When the lifeboat bell is sounded, passengers put on their lifejackets, go to their boat stations, and wait for orders. Boat drills and safety drills for the crew occur routinely during world cruises. A lifejacket from the S.S. United States. $85.

Soaps used aboard Cunard and the Peter Deilmann ships. In the 1970s and 1980s, Cunard used plastic soap containers. In the 1990s, the line switched to cardboard boxes. Notice the constantly changing lion logo. $5 each.

An aluminum vase used on the S.S. United States showing the eagle insignia. The United States was touted as a fireproof ship and this vase, as well as most on-board furnishings, including deck chairs, were made of aluminum. $250.

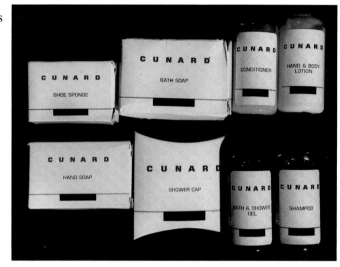

Soaps and bottles of lotions used aboard QE2 in 1997. $5 each.

Matches used aboard the Royal Viking Sun in 1997 carry the Royal Viking Sun sea eagle logo. $2.

While there is little value for small items such as soaps, stationary, cocktail napkins, or baggage tags taken from modern ships, like all ship memorabilia, in time these bits and pieces will assume more and more value. We are strong advocates of preservation and are increasingly grateful to all those dedicated travelers who have saved all their ephemera—tickets, bills, luggage tags, passenger lists, and menus. Old photo albums contain hundreds of dollars worth of ship stuff coveted by collectors, as well as a detailed visual history of the great liners. Pictured are cabin breakfast menus, stationary, package tags, and a key used aboard the Royal Viking Sun in 1997. $2 each.

A Royal Viking Sun cabin breakfast menu. $2.

While to some it may seem silly to save stationery, unused mint condition stationery from the Lusitania sells for as much as $65; unused Baltic stationary for $25; Berengaria stationary with its crest sells for $15; Rex stationary with an imperial crest in gold for $65; stationary from the Normandie for $45, and Normandie notecards for $35. Letters range in value depending on ship, date, or the people who wrote or received the letters. For example maiden voyage or disaster letters have additional value. Stationery from the S.S. United States, the France, Queen Elizabeth 2, Cunard Sea Goddess, and the QE2's world cruise. $2-$10.

Stationery used aboard the Vistafjord. $2.

A welcome aboard card from the United States. $5.

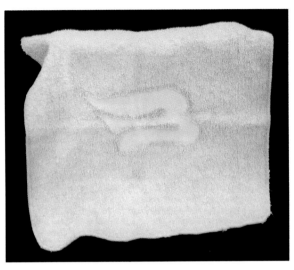

"My Voyage, Facts and Figures," a souvenir book handed out on the Queen Elizabeth. $25.

A hand towel from the Royal Viking Sun with the sea eagle logo. $5.

An Italian Line towel. $25.

A room service place mat used aboard the Italian Line's Saturnia. This was probably for a special luncheon event in Venice. $40.

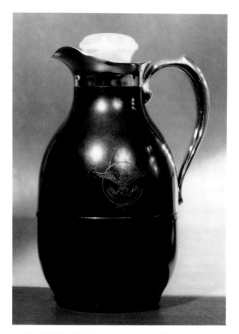

A rotary telephone used on the United States. It has the eagle logo on the back. $125.

In 1984, all the contents of the United States were auctioned off in a giant sale at Norfolk, Virginia. Boxes of china, glassware, silver, telephones, and room furnishings were carried off by dealers and collectors. A bakelite water thermos used in the cabins of the United States. $200.

A cabin on the Royal Viking Sun's One Deck with its own balcony.

An early 1900s notepad used on the North German Lloyd liner Bremen. $35.

Chapter 5

Inside the Dining Room

Menus, China, Kosher Service, Glass, and Silver

Dickens described the dining room aboard the Britannia as "a gigantic hearse with windows." Twentieth century passengers would describe latter-day dining rooms in more elegant and ecstatic terms.

The 1884–'85 Cunarders Umbria and Etruria were the first ships to have refrigerated food service on board, an improvement on the Britannia, which boasted the on-board presence of a cow to provide fresh milk.

Cunard advertised that the 1893 Campania and Lucania were "a silent sermon in good taste." They had revolving chairs in the restaurant and gilded pipes in the organ.

In 1903, Albert Ballin was the first shipping line director to institute an *a la carte* grill restaurant on board the Amerika and lured the distinguished Caesar Ritz of the Ritz in Paris as head of his restaurant. This was a major innovation and marked the beginning of a new age in shipboard cuisine.

Ballin boasted that his ships could feed his passengers at all hours for an additional charge. His wait-staff was considered one of the best at sea.

Ballin ran a very tight ship and routinely cruised aboard the ships of the Hamburg-Amerika line. One of his early memos noted that the 11 a.m. bouillon was good but there needed to be an improvement in the cup design to prevent spilling on the passengers when there were rough seas.

Ballin sparked a new race in ocean liner design and soon his ships and Cunard's Lusitania and Mauretania boasted that they had passenger accommodations and dining facilities comparable to the best hotels of the day.

The dining room was not only a place to eat, but a public room in which to socialize and find companionship. It was also designed to be more spacious and have more light than the cabins, which were often cramped and dreary. Since the most important part of ship life was the evening meal, restaurant design became a very important matter.

The Kaiserin Auguste Victoria introduced the first grill room to its first class passengers. Until then passengers were served their meals either at long galley tables or at smaller tables reminiscent of boarding-house styles.

The Olympic was the first ship to allow tables for two. Before that, first class was seated at long, narrow dining tables.

The variety of foods served on board ships have been a tribute to man's ingenuity and inventiveness as well as the scientific advances in refrigeration. Early ship dining rooms served mostly preserved foods. The American Collins Line ships were the first to serve fresh food. Their ice rooms had a capacity of forty tons of frozen water. It was estimated that it would take fourteen days before the ice thawed.

Aboard the ship the Atlantic, fresh fish was always one of the nine courses. In addition, its kitchen boasted that there were always at least forty other items available. The Collins Line served turtle soup, fresh lobster, goose in champagne sauce, and a period specialty—fillet of zander, a kind of waterfowl.

The French Line had large, spacious staircases leading into the dining room as early as the 1919 Paris. The restaurant of the Ile de France had angular, steel-tubed furniture and laquered panels. The first-class dining room rose three decks in height.

The Normandie dining room had bronze hammered glass and Lalique glass fixtures. It could seat a thousand diners at a time, and it also rose three decks high. In the 1960s, the Chambord Restaurant on the France was a circular design with an imposing center staircase entrance. The Holland America's Nieuw Amsterdam's main restaurant had ivory glass, pale gold ceilings, and columns covered with gold leaf. The United States had magnificent aluminum alloy sculptures on the walls of the dining room.

Life on board ship is an experience few can imagine unless lucky enough to try it. In 1939, Cunard advertised that Queen Mary carried more than a half-million pieces of china, silver, and glassware. In addition, for each voyage it stocked 210,000 towels, 30,000 sheets, 31,000 pillow cases, 21,000 cloths and 92,000 napkins. On a round-trip its provisions included 1,000 pineapples, 2,000 quarts of ice cream, twenty tons of meat, 60,000 eggs, six tons of fresh fish, 850 pounds of tea, 1,200 pounds of coffee, 3,600 pounds of butter, and the obligatory twenty-four unsinkable lifeboats.

The 1842 Britannia carried 200 passengers. The 1939 Queen Mary carried 2,075.

Both the Queen Mary and the Queen Elizabeth, which finally returned to commercial service in 1946 after years of wartime service, had an a la carte grill available at an additional cost for those first-class passengers requiring privacy. Tables here were coveted by the rich, the famous, the illustrious, and the many movie stars who sailed frequently.

One of the most stunning aspects of the Verandah Grill on the Queen Mary was its jet black carpet.

Since the Queen Mary, all Cunard dining rooms have had only one exit. This came about at the suggestion of maitre d' of the Queen Mary, who found that it was impossible to greet all departing passengers with the Mary's double-door exit. With only one exit, it was easier for the maitre d' to greet all passengers and bid them good-bye. Thus assuring that he would receive all his rightful tips.

I still remember the luxurious setting of the Mauretania restaurant, the QE2's first-class dining room, in 1974 when a young waiter arrived at our table with a magnificent silver trolley and slowly sliced the smoked salmon by hand, with large sweeping graceful strokes.

I also remember the thrill each night of descending down the grand staircase into the Chambord, the first-class restaurant of the France, and walking past buffet tables covered with ice sculptures, serving tables decorated with small pastel candy pianos, and more tables strewn with dramatic sweeps of floating, fondant candy ribbons.

Today's passengers assume that they are immune from the raging seas because of the presence of stabilizers, but older travelers still remember the days when dining-room stewards would dampen the tablecloths during heavy storms and raise small rimmed gates from underneath each table in heavy seas to keep the plates, glasses, and silverware from flying off onto the floor.

China and menus are among the most popular ocean liner collectibles. Of the two, menus are the most abundant and the most affordable, often ranging in price from $10 to $50.

Menus not only offer vicarious thrills and pleasure, they are also fascinating to read. They are fun as historic documents, useful as culinary inspiration, and often are artistic treasures.

In 1997 when the Halcyon Restaurant in New York City announced it would remember the 85th anniversary of the sinking of the Titanic and attempt to duplicate the last meal served aboard its a-la-carte restaurant, it was swamped with reservations. The one-night event became a two-day celebration as twentieth century diners tried to keep up with the gargantuan appetites of the original White Star passengers.

Menu covers also have artistic and historic interest. Some lines duplicated classic works of art. The Italian liner Raffaello used some of Raphael's famous portraits as menu covers. The Moore-McCormack line commissioned original art. Cunard duplicated famous English artwork or illustrated historically important locations or events. Other Cunard covers trace the famous Cunard lineage and show some of the early flag bearers of the Cunard fleet.

The French line commissioned a series by the French artist, Jean Mercier, depicting traditional French folk songs, classical French poetry, and charming period vignettes. French Line menus are so collectible that many now hang in some of the leading restaurants of the world as well as in the private dining rooms of former passengers.

Some menu connoisseurs even collect by artist. The Matson Line menus are particularly popular because of their originality and freshness of design.

Entire books could be devoted to the art of the menu. Each line commissioned original works of art or developed unique nationalistic themes such as the costume series aboard the French Line. The early White Star lines used expensive paper for their menus. Some of the early Hamburg-Amerika menus were hand painted.

China, glassware, and silver are more expensive collectibles. They, too, recall a time when dining was an art and people spent a lot of time planning elaborately set tables with full china, silver, and glass service. The first-class dining rooms on Titanic used four different patterns of china.

The Victorians had enormous appetites. An 1894 menu on RMSS Danube-Royal Mail Service offered a sumptuous breakfast featuring cheese straws, sardines, vegetable soup, fried fish, Beef Portuguese, spaghetti parmesan, mutton, and walnuts.

A dinner on the 1910 R.M.S. Majestic might include cold consommé, pea soup, fresh lobsters, potted shrimps, salmon cakes, pigs' cheeks and cabbage, vegetable stew, grilled mutton, or rolled ox tongue.

An April 14, 1912 a la carte diner on the Titanic could have eaten consommé olga, salmon mousseline sauce with cucumbers, filet mignon, sauté of chicken lyonnaise, vegetable marrow farcie, lamb with mint sauce, roast duckling with apple sauce, and sirloin of beef with chateau potatoes.

A 1913 menu from the Carmania suggested a choice of Green Turtle soup, filet de sole meuniere, noisettes d'agneau au lait, parisienne caneton d'Ayelesbury, and assiettes of lamb.

A 1927 U.S. Leviathan tourist-class menu offered boiled weakfish sauce Hollandaise, leg of lamb with mint sauce, roast turkey with cranberry sauce, and American ice cream cake.

The 1927 S.S. Republic served boiled halibut with oyster sauce, fried yellow perch in brown butter, calf's feet a la Delmonico or timbale of capon a la Heredia, or breakfast of oatmeal porridge, rolled oats, fried sole, tartar sauce, kippered herrings, scotch pancakes to order from the silver grill, beefsteaks, mutton chops, York ham, and grilled kidney.

Aboard the 1929 Ile de France, luncheon could be blue point oysters, brochettes of smelts in tartar sauce, small sausages, or calf kidneys in cocotte

The 1933 Bremen offered North German herring salad, cream of asparagus soup with egg custard, poached codfish, goose liver dumplings, sweetbreads on toast, okra with tomatoes, and a special Manhattan clam chowder

An October 11, 1951, dinner on the Mauretania began with potage St. Louis, turtle soup with sherry, fillet of flounder Cleopatra, rack of lamb, and roast Long Island duckling and ended with a meringue with strawberries, a coupe Venus, and Soufflé Rothschild.

Another 1953 gala shipboard dinner began with tortellini in double consommé, lobster with a ravigotte sauce, calf's brain medallion, and stewed poularde. This is rather more opulent than a 1953 cabin class luncheon on the Andrea Doria, which offered short-cut macaroni with Bolognese sauce, boiled grayling and kidney, and bacon with tomatoes.

A 1953 farewell dinner on the Andrea Doria was more elaborate. It began with a terrine of truffled foie gras, a white lady cream soup, pojarsky of veal, and spring turkey on a skewer.

A July 1954 Liberte lunch offered rack of lamb a la mode, calves liver, poached broccoli hollandaise, braised heart of celery with marrow, and fresh corn a la hongroise, gnocchi, "short horn" prime ribs, or broiled young pigeon.

A 1959 luncheon on Queen Mary included Manhattan clam chowder, cold lobsters, calf liver sautéed with French fried onions, mulligatawny soup, crab salad, and chicken with risotto.

A dinner aboard the first Queen Elizabeth began with cold sorrel soup, potage solferino, poached filets of halibut dieppoise, lamb chops, frog legs, pigeon en cocotte, veal, sweetbreads basted with julienne of vegetables carrots, leeks, celery moistened with veal stock served in cocotte with julienne of vegetables, and slices of truffles.

A May 19, 1969, cruise on the Moore-McCormack's S.S. Argentina served cherrystone clams, cream of cauliflower, and vichyssoise soups, smoked ox tongue, and prime rib au jus. The featured special of that meal was boneless Cornish game hen with a special fois gras dressing.

A gala dinner on the United States in October 1969 served fresh Alaska crab meat cocktail, foie gras with melba toast, clear green turtle soup, curried shrimp Bombay, a bone-in sirloin steak, Vienna mocha layer cake, and French ice cream.

A 1996 captain's dinner on Royal Viking Sun offered lobster cocktail with Cognac Chantilly, and caviar, celery cream soup with spinach quenelles, Greek salad with feta cheese and olives, roast duckling a la orange with caramelized red cabbage, crepes with vanilla ice cream and coffee sauce, and old fashioned pumpkin pie. In addition, two wines were served: a Chateau Carbonnieux, Grand Cru Classe 1992, and a Chateau Batailley, Fifth Growth 1989.

A 1997 captain's dinner aboard the Royal Viking Sun began with caviar and goose livers followed by fresh Canadian lobsters and Kansas Rib Eye Steak as a main course.

Today's ships offer, besides the regular meal, a vegetarian selection and a complete spa menu complete with a listing of calories. Weight-conscious diners can dine regally each day on 1,500 calories, ordering from Golden Door Spa-designed menus, which include such luscious desserts as kiwi or papaya mousse, non-fat ice-creams, and low-calorie cookies.

Room service has always been part of shipboard life. Besides breakfast in bed at no additional cost, passengers can order off the menu nearly twenty-four hours a day. On a summer arctic cruise in the land of the Midnight Sun, Vistafjord chefs offered twenty-four-hour room service, which included fresh pizzas, sandwiches, fruit, cheese, and minute steaks.

In the early twentieth century, all of the exclusively male ship wait-staff wore white gloves and were formally dressed. Today, while most waiters are still formally dressed, many ships have male and female wait staff. The Royal Viking Sun still has an all-male wait-staff.

While shipboard cuisine has always been international in concept, most German ships would feature German specialties, French ships would specialize in French, and the English would serve traditional English foods such as roasts, steak and kidney pies, and savories. Usually, most ships would include an American dish, such as Manhattan clam chowder, Long Island duckling, or an ice cream dessert as a specialty.

Through the years shipping lines vied with one another to create more elaborate and sumptuous bills of fare. The S.S. France was considered to be the finest French restaurant in the world.

On a recent trip aboard the German based Peter Deilmann EuropAmerica Line, bratwurst, beer, and homemade pretzels were served on deck and red cabbage, spaetzle, and goose fat and pork were on the menus daily.

The Bergen Line served daily buffets of herring, shrimp; Barents Sea salmon both fresh, pickled, and smoked; reindeer, and arctic caviar.

Years ago, QE2 served heavy British specialties such as steak and kidney pies, roasts, and mutton. Today QE2 serves lighter and better-seasoned foods, and English specialties like roasts, grills, mutton, oxtail, and steak and kidney pie can be special ordered.

I recall one cruise in which one first-class passenger arrived with his own oxtail so that he could be assured of having fresh braised oxtail, and oxtail soup. And, of course, the chef willingly obliged.

Today on QE2, twenty percent of all passengers routinely order caviar, lobster, Beef Wellington, or rack of lamb off the menu each day at no extra charge. But while the menu lists six elaborate courses each night, most people order only two or three, and fish is more popular than beef.

A 1890s ticket for first-class passage on the White Star R.M.S. Teutonic. $50.

The Normandie's grand dining room. The statue in the center is now in the Fontainebleau Hotel in Miami.

A first-class place setting on the Normandie. The glasses are by Lalique, the silver is by Christolfe, and the china is Limoges with a special pattern designed by Jean Luce.

A tea place setting in the first-class Queen's Grill on QE2. The china is all special order Royal Doulton.

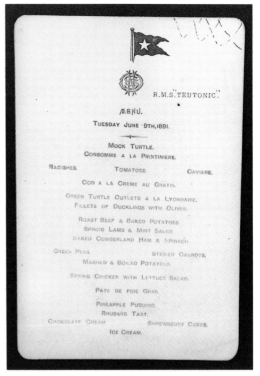

A menu from the White Star Royal Mail Steamer Teutonic with the same Oceanic Steam and Navigation logo. $30.

A small saucer used on the Oceanic Steam and Navigation Company, which was the corporate name of White Star and was later acquired by J. P. Morgan's Intermerchantile Navigation Co. Note the logo. $35.

A 1891 menu used on the Inman and International Steamship Company Limited R.M.S. City of Paris. $35.

A 1902 hand-written breakfast menu from the R.M.S.S. Danube. $35.

An 1890s Hamburg Amerika Line menu cover. $35.

Often passengers would tear off the tops of menus and use them as postcards to write home. A colorful fold-over Hamburg Amerika Line menu from the late 1890s or early 1900s. $40

A 1907 Allan Line menu from the R.M.S. Victorian. This is from a page in a 1900s travel album. $30.

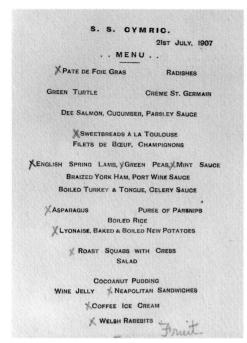

S. S. CYMRIC.

21st July, 1907

. . M E N U . .

Pate de Foie Gras   Radishes

Green Turtle   Crème St. Germain

Dee Salmon, Cucumber, Parsley Sauce

Sweetbreads à la Toulouse
Filets de Bœuf, Champignons

English Spring Lamb, Green Peas, Mint Sauce
Braized York Ham, Port Wine Sauce
Boiled Turkey & Tongue, Celery Sauce

Asparagus   Puree of Parsnips
Boiled Rice
Lyonaise, Baked & Boiled New Potatoes

Roast Squabs with Cress
Salad

Cocoanut Pudding
Wine Jelly   Neapolitan Sandwiches

Coffee Ice Cream

Welsh Rarebits   *Fruit*

A 1907 menu from the White Star liner Cymric. Notice the custom of serving a savory such as Welsh Rarebits after the dessert. Serving savories remained a common practice on English ships through the 1970s. They are no longer listed on Cunard's menus, but can be special ordered. $25.

WHITE STAR LINE.

R.M.S. OCEANIC.

2ND CLASS.

May 13th, 1908

Consomme Printanier

Boiled Cod, Egg Sauce

Beefsteak & Kidney Pudding

Roast Mutton, Browned Potatoes
Boiled Fowl & Bacon, Cream Sauce

Cauliflower
Vegetable Marrow
Browned & Boiled Potatoes

Sago Pudding
Chester Cake   Ice Cream

Fruit   Cheese
Nuts

Coffee

A 1908 second-class menu used on the White Star Oceanic. Steak and kidney puddings remained on the menu on the Cunard liners through the 1970s. Today they are served only by special order. $25.

A 1909 North German Lloyd menu from the Bremen. $30.

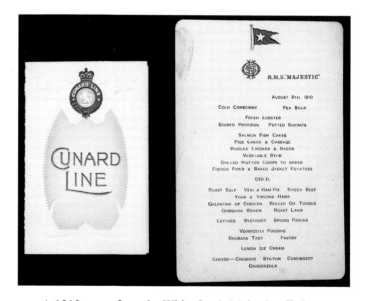

A 1910 menu from the White Star's Majestic offering fresh lobster, pig's cheek and cabbage, and grilled mutton chops to order. This small 2- by 3-inch card is the same size as those used on the Titanic. Note again the O.S.N.C. logo. $35.

A 1913 Cunard Line Carmania embossed menu cover. $45.

A 1927 menu from the United States Shipping Lines' S.S. Republic. Notice that passengers are requested not to smoke in the Dining Saloon. For many years smoking was restricted to the smoking room, which was a private male sanctum. With the coming of age of women during the 1920s and 1930s, it was no longer considered immoral or outrageous for women to smoke in public and smoking was allowed in all the public rooms of restaurants, hotels, and ocean liners. Today smoking is once again restricted to smoking areas and many ships now have special smoking rooms where men and women can enjoy a cigarette or cigar without offending non-smokers. $35.

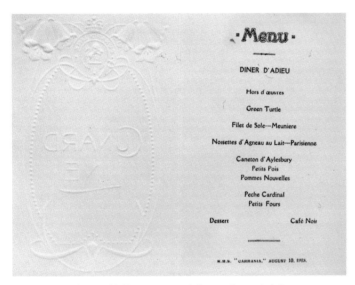

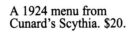

Inside the farewell dinner menu (pictured top right).

A 1924 menu from Cunard's Scythia. $20.

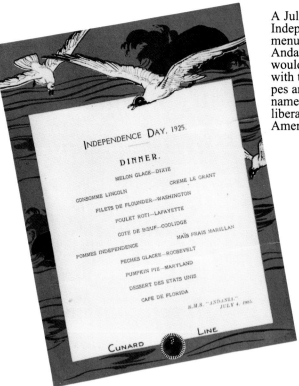

A July 4th 1925 Independence Day menu on Cunard's Andania. Often chefs would take liberties with traditional recipes and give them new names. Notice the liberal sprinkling of Americana. $25.

INDEPENDENCE DAY. 1925.

DINNER.

MELON GLACE—DIXIE

CONSOMME LINCOLN   CREME LE GRANT

FILETS DE FLOUNDER—WASHINGTON

POULET ROTI—LAFAYETTE

COTE DE BŒUF—COOLIDGE

MAÏS FRAIS MARILLAN

POMMES INDEPENDENCE

PECHES GLACEE—ROOSEVELT

PUMPKIN PIE—MARYLAND

DESSERT DES ETATS UNIS

CAFE DE FLORIDA

R.M.S. "ANDANIA."
JULY 4, 1925.

CUNARD LINE

CUNARD LINE

River Procession at Queen Elizabeth's Coronation, 1559.

R.M.S. BERENGARIA.   THURSDAY, JULY 30, 1925.

FAREWELL DINNER.

Grape Fruit

Consomme Alphabet   Lentil Soup

Boiled Halibut—Dutch Sauce

Roast Turkey—Cranberry Sauce

Baked York Ham

Cauliflower a la Creme

Roast and Boiled Potatoes

Semolina Pudding

Ice Cream   Wafers

Rolls and Butter   Coffee

A cover of a 1925 Farewell Dinner menu from the Berengaria depicting the 1559 coronation of Queen Elizabeth 1. $20.

A Leviathan menu cover with an illustration of the Pilgrim's ship, the Mayflower. $25.

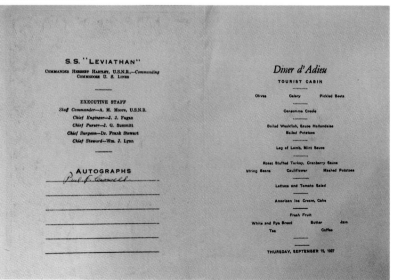

A 1927 Tourist cabin-class farewell dinner menu. $25.

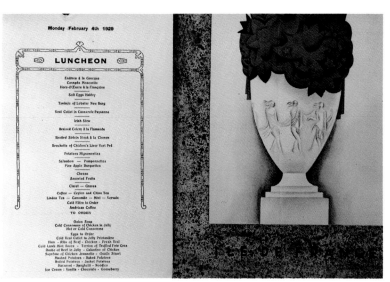

A 1929 luncheon menu from the French Line's Ile de France. $30.

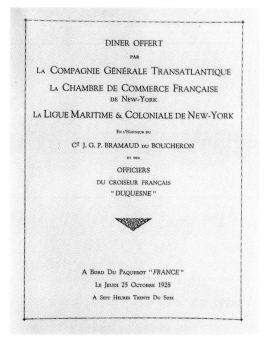

DINER OFFERT

PAR

LA COMPAGNIE GÉNÉRALE TRANSATLANTIQUE

LA CHAMBRE DE COMMERCE FRANÇAISE
DE NEW-YORK

LA LIGUE MARITIME & COLONIALE DE NEW-YORK

EN L'HONNEUR DU

Cᵗ J. G. P. BRAMAUD DU BOUCHERON

ET DES

OFFICIERS

DU CROISEUR FRANÇAIS
"DUQUESNE"

A BORD DU PAQUEBOT "FRANCE"
LE JEUDI 25 OCTOBRE 1928
A SEPT HEURES TRENTE DU SOIR

A 1928 private dinner given aboard the first France. $15.

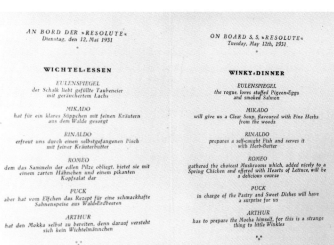

A 1931 menu for a "Winky Dinner" aboard the Resolute with "tongue in cheek" descriptions of the food. $20.

A 1937 Normandie tourist-class luncheon menu. $75.

A 1974 dinner menu from the Chambord restaurant, the first-class restaurant on the France. This crossing was the last westbound crossing of the France. On her return to Le Havre, her crew mutinied and refused to land. $25.

L'ALOUETTE

Compagnie G...
g...

A Jean Mercier illus-
tration of Ronsard's
poem "A Sa
Maitresse" on a 1974
France dinner menu.
The words of the
poem are on the
reverse cover. $25.

...aie Générale Transatlantique
French Line

A 1972 luncheon m...
lyrics of the French...
is on the reverse. T...
original illustration...
Mercier used on th...

AH! VOUS...
MAMAN

EUT BERGÈRE

Compagnie Générale Transatlantique

"Il Pleut Bergere," another Mercier illustration for
a 1950s Liberte luncheon menu. $15.

"Ah! Vous Dirais Je Maman," a 1954 luncheon
menu from the Liberte. These menus have
become highly collectible and many have been
framed and hung ashore in both public and
private dining rooms. $15.

Another 1974 France menu. $25

A luncheon menu for the France from September 1974. $25.

A 1947 dinner menu from the Queen Elizabeth. $15.

"J'ai du Bon Tabac," a July 1954 Liberte luncheon menu. $15.

A 1947 Queen Elizabeth luncheon menu with a portrait of King James II on the cover. The original was painted by Geoffrey Kneller and hung in the smoking room of the Aquitania. $15.

"Auld Lang Syne, a 1947 farewell dinner menu from the Queen Elizabeth. $15.

A 1947 Queen Elizabeth luncheon menu. $10.

A 1947 dinner menu from the Queen Elizabeth. $15.

A 1947 luncheon menu from the Queen Elizabeth showing the mounted guards leaving Buckingham Palace. $15.

A 1947 Queen Elizabeth luncheon menu cover. The cover is a copy of Philip Connard's painting *Merrie England*, which hung in the restaurant on the Queen Mary. $15.

Both the luncheon menu cover shown above and this 1947 dinner menu from the Queen Elizabeth were wonderful works of art. $15.

A 1959 gala dinner menu decorated with a woven green cord from the Queen Elizabeth. $15.

A Cunard/White Star menu showing the Cunard/White Star logo—a ship with a crown. Under the portrait of the Queen Elizabeth are the words "The world's largest Liner," a claim made by every line at one time or another. $10.

The cover of this 1959 Queen Elizabeth dinner menu cover shows a carpet embroidered by Queen Mary. It took the Queen from 1942–1950 to complete it. When it was completed, she presented it to the British people. The carpet crossed the Atlantic on the Queen Mary, toured the United States, and found a permanent home in the National Gallery of Canada in Ottawa. $25.

A 1959 luncheon menu from the Queen Elizabeth. $10.

A 1959 Queen Elizabeth luncheon menu with a poem by John Milton on the reverse. $10.

Lac d'Annecy. A 1959 luncheon menu on the Queen Elizabeth. $20. Cunard menu covers had nautical, historic, and geographical themes. Cunard has discontinued the practice of using individual menu covers at each meal. Now each passenger is given a packet of menus under one generic cover at the end of the voyage. $10.

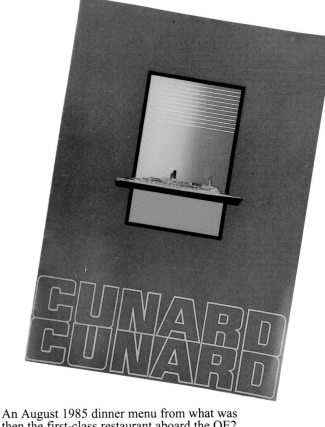

This 1959 Queen Elizabeth luncheon menu pictures Harvard House, the birthplace of Alice Rogers, John Harvard's mother. Harvard later founded Harvard College in Massachusetts. The half-timbered Tudor-style house was built in 1596 by Harvard's grandparents on High Street in Stratford-upon-Avon and is now the property of Harvard University. $25.

An August 1985 dinner menu from what was then the first-class restaurant aboard the QE2, the Columbia. This voyage was one of the first times that QE2 sailed from New York to Boston, taking on a large contingent of Irish in Boston. Because of the difficulties in Ireland, security was very tight when the ship arrived in Boston harbor and no one was allowed off the ship without an official okay except the author, who had an emergency dental problem and was treated immediately by a Boston dentist. While ships have a doctor aboard, few have a trained dentist. $20.

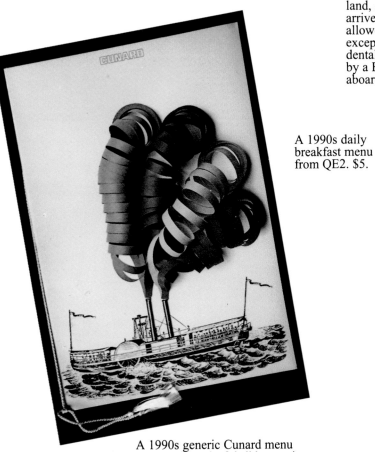

A 1990s daily breakfast menu from QE2. $5.

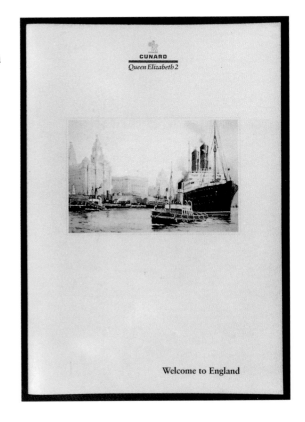

A 1990s generic Cunard menu cover, with colorful ribbons, given out at the end of the voyage. $10.

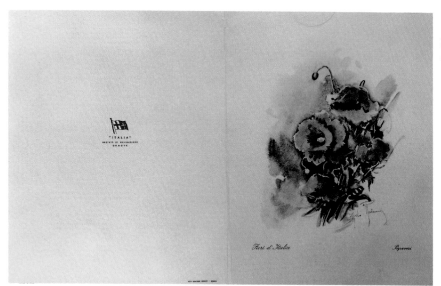

A 1953 Andrea Doria cabin-class dinner menu. Traditionally cabin-class menus have less value than those of first class. $30.

A gala cabin-class dinner menu from the Italian Line's Andrea Doria. $25.

An 1933 a la carte lunch menu from North German Lloyd's S.S. Bremen. $15.

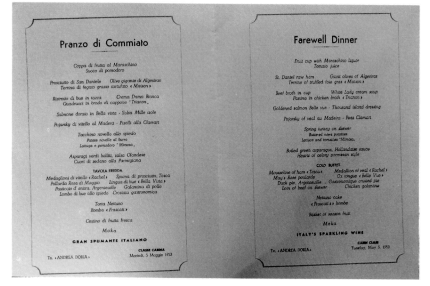

Even a cabin-class passenger ate sumptuously aboard the Andrea Doria.

A 1969 Moore-McCormack S.S. Argentina dinner menu from a Caribbean cruise. On the back of the cover is a world map showing Moore-McCormack destinations. $10.

Another 1969 Moore-McCormack S.S. Argentina's dinner menu. The painting on the cover, *Native Trinidad Scene*, was painted for Moore-McCormack by Pierre Belliveau. $10.

An Independence Day menu bound with a gold elastic cord from a 1992 voyage on QE2 showing a new Cunard logo—a Cunard lion spanning the globe. Since then Trafalger House Company, the London-based conglomerate that owned Cunard in the 1980s, has sold the company to a Norwegian-based conglomerate. On Nov. 28, 1997, Cunard left its longtime New York City headquarters and moved to their new base in Miami. $5.

This S.S. Argentina menu cover, *Midnight Sun of the Vikings*, was an original work of art painted by Mary Moran for Moore-McCormack. $10.

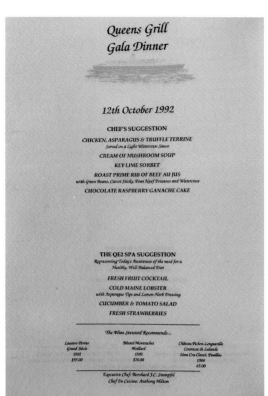

Queens Grill
Gala Dinner

12th October 1992

CHEF'S SUGGESTION

CHICKEN, ASPARAGUS & TRUFFLE TERRINE
Served on a Light Watercress Sauce

CREAM OF MUSHROOM SOUP

KEY LIME SORBET

ROAST PRIME RIB OF BEEF AU JUS
with Green Beans, Carrot Sticks, Pont Neuf Potatoes and Watercress

CHOCOLATE RASPBERRY GANACHE CAKE

THE QE2 SPA SUGGESTION
Representing Today's Awareness of the need for a
Healthy, Well-Balanced Diet

FRESH FRUIT COCKTAIL

COLD MAINE LOBSTER
with Asparagus Tips and Lemon Herb Dressing

CUCUMBER & TOMATO SALAD

FRESH STRAWBERRIES

The Wine Steward Recommends...

| Laurent Perrier Grand Siècle 1982 $95.00 | Bâtard-Montrachet Moillard 1980 $70.00 | Château Pichon-Longueville Comtesse de Lalande 2ème Cru Classé, Pauillac 1984 65.00 |

Executive Chef: Bernhard J.C. Stumpfel
Chef De Cuisine: Anthony Milton

An October 12, 1992 Queen's Grill gala dinner menu. $3.

A June 16th, 1995 gala dinner menu celebrating QE2's thousandth voyage. The meal began with iced Russian caviar and fresh cold Maine lobster. $10.

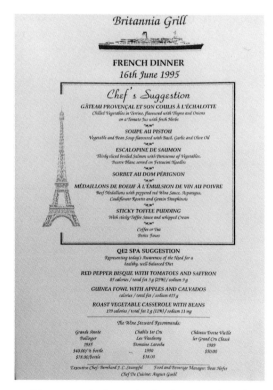

Britannia Grill

FRENCH DINNER
16th June 1995

Chef's Suggestion

GÂTEAU PROVENÇAL ET SON COULIS À L'ÉCHALOTTE
Chilled Vegetables in Terrine, flavoured with Thyme and Onions
on a Tomato Jus with fresh Herbs

SOUPE AU PISTOU
Vegetable and Bean Soup flavoured with Basil, Garlic and Olive Oil

ESCALOPINE DE SAUMON
Thinly sliced broiled Salmon with Parisienne of Vegetables,
Beurre Blanc served on Fettucini Noodles

SORBET AU DOM PÉRIGNON

MÉDAILLONS DE BOEUF À L'ÉMULSION DE VIN AU POIVRE
Beef Medallions with peppered red Wine Sauce, Asparagus,
Cauliflower Rosette and Gratin Dauphinois

STICKY TOFFEE PUDDING
With sticky Toffee Sauce and whipped Cream

Coffee or Tea
Petits Fours

QE2 SPA SUGGESTION
Representing today's Awareness of the Need for a
healthy, well-balanced Diet

RED PEPPER BISQUE WITH TOMATOES AND SAFFRON
85 calories / total fat 3 g (29%) / sodium 9 g

GUINEA FOWL WITH APPLES AND CALVADOS
calories / total fat / sodium 415 g

ROAST VEGETABLE CASSEROLE WITH BEANS
199 calories / total fat 2 g (11%) / sodium 11 mg

The Wine Steward Recommends:

| Grande Année Bollinger 1985 $40.00/½ bottle $78.00/bottle | Chablis 1er Cru Les Vaudevey Domaine Laroche 1990 $38.00 | Château Trotte Vieille 1er Grand Cru Classé 1989 $50.00 |

Executive Chef: Bernhard J. C. Stumpfel   Food and Beverage Manager: Beat Hofer
Chef De Cuisine: August Goebl

A 1995 French dinner in the QE2's Britannia Grill featuring elaborate French-inspired cuisine. The Britannia Grill is one of the three grill rooms aboard QE2. The other two are the Queen's and the Princess Grill. $3.

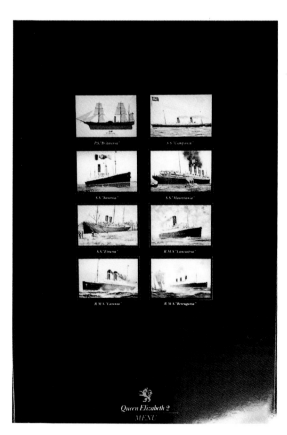

Generic 1990s QE2 menu covers. $5.

A Matson Line menu cover. $45.

A United States 1969 gala dinner menu. $20.

An American President Line menu cover. $15.

A 1969 farewell dinner menu aboard the Raffaello. $20.

A 1969 Mediterranean cruise dinner menu on the Raffaello. $20.

Another 1969 Raffaello menu cover. $20.

A 1953 cabin-class menu from the Andrea Doria. $20.

An American President Lines' menu. $10.

A 1930s menu from the United States Lines. $30.

A 1990s menu from the Peter Deilmann EuropAmerica cruises. $5.

Lard sculptures from the buffet table on the Royal Viking Sun on a voyage from Bombay to Singapore.

A menu from the Rotterdam's final voyage in September 1997. $5 (Will probably be worth much more within ten years.)

A first-class place setting on the Queen Mary. The Mary was considered the epitome of oceangoing elegance. The cube-shaped tea service was designed for balance in rough seas. The china was designed by Foley bone china of Liverpool. Later Wedgwood and Royal Doulton would manufacture Cunard china.

Although this Lancaster china jam pot comes with a silver-plated lid stamped with the name "Laconia," its provenance may be questionable. It has been suggested that the lid is authentic and the china is a period piece, but whether the two go together is not known. $65.

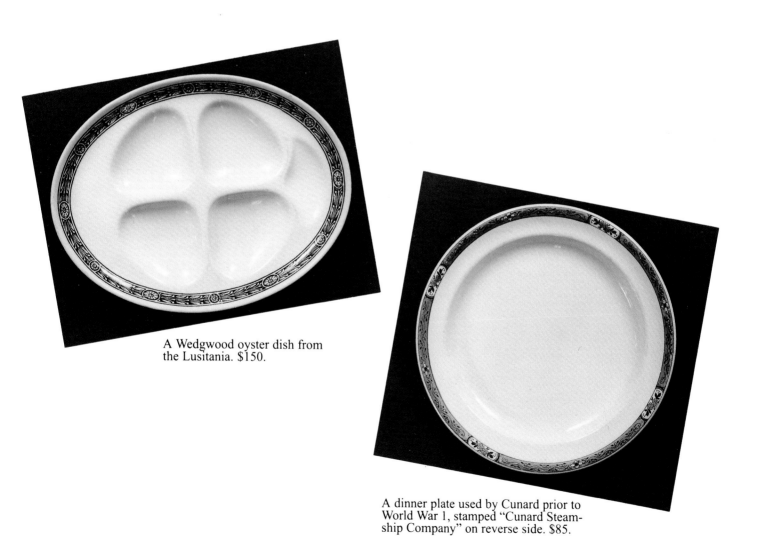

A Wedgwood oyster dish from the Lusitania. $150.

A dinner plate used by Cunard prior to World War 1, stamped "Cunard Steamship Company" on reverse side. $85.

A kosher milk plate from QE2. $50.

China with the bird of paradise design was used on the Aquitania and the Mauretania. $50.

A dinner plate used on the Mauretania, the Aquitania, and, in its early years, the Queen Mary. $130.

A Wedgwood coffee cup and saucer used in the early years of QE2 in the Queen's Grill. Currently used in the Princess and Britannic Grills and the Coronia Restaurant.

The Queen Mary's Verandah Grill was a deluxe a la carte restaurant open to first-class passengers at an additional fee. Cunard has continued the idea of an exclusive grill experience and today has three grills on QE2. In the 1980s, Queen's Grill was available to all first-class passengers at an extra fee. Today it is only for passengers on the top two decks.

A Wedgwood cup and saucer from QE2's Queen's Grill in the 1970s and 1980s (by 1997 this pattern was only used in the Princess and Britannic Grills and the Caronia restaurants). A cup from the S.S. United States with the star pattern, $50. A Royal Doulton cup from QE2's Queen's Grill. A Peter Deilmann cup, $20. The generic pattern used today on QE2 and Royal Viking Sun's Lido deck buffet.

A 1900s plate with the White Star logo. $350.

An International Mercantile Marine plate used on one of J. P. Morgan's ships. $150.

A pre-World War I blue and white china plate used aboard the White Star fleet. $400.

A cup and saucer in the floral bird-of-paradise pattern used aboard the Aquitania and the Mauretania, $75. The cup is marked "souvenir" on the bottom and was sold in the on-board gift shop.

The cubed coffee and tea service used on the Queen Mary. This pale striped pattern was used in the first-class restaurants. $450.

A plate used on the Matson Line. $125.

A second-class porcelain dinner plate from the Lusitania. This design originated in the nineteenth century when it was used in the first-class dining room on the Campania. The Campania plates also came in a beige-rose pattern. This blue-and-white pattern was used on Cunard ships in the early twentieth century. $450.

A plate from the tea service of the Italian line's Augustus from the 1920s. Note the logo. Before World War II, the logo had a more decorative crown and the name Italia was in script. After the war, the crown took on a modern look and the name Italia was written in capital letters. The Italian Line marked all ship stuff "Italia." $300.

Pre-war Italia line china used aboard Guilio Cesare and the Augustus. $300.

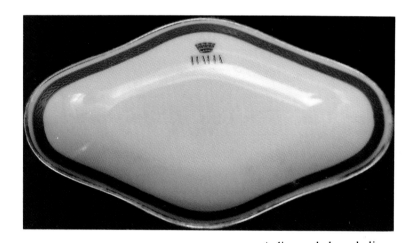

A diamond-shaped olive dish used on the Andrea Doria. Note the new crown logo on top, the gold and reddish woven pattern. Italian lines generally did not use the name of the individual ships. $100. In the 1950s the Italian line also used a blue and gold pattern that was similar. $85.

A pre-war dessert plate in the Cockerel pattern used in the Grill Room of the Italian line's "Rex." This is pre-war because after the war the crown logo was changed. Richard Ginori designed many beautiful china patterns for the Italian liners. $300. There is also a cup and saucer in this pattern: $375, and crystal stemware: $200 each.

Another beautiful Ginori plate used on the Italian liners the Michelangelo and the Raffaello. $100.

A cup and saucer from the Japanese N.Y.K. (Nippon Yusen Kaisha) Line. $75.

A first-class place setting on the Normandie. The china was designed by Jean Luce, the silverware by Christolfe, the glasses by Lalique.

A creamer used on the HAPAG line. $45.

An egg cup used aboard the French Line and probably the Normandie. $65.

A plate used in first-class on the Normandie. This was designed by Jean Luce for Limoges. $400.

Egg cups used aboard the QE2, United States, and the Royal Viking Sun. $50 for the United States egg cup.

A Lalique goblet from the Normandie. $500

A complete set of Lalique glasses from the Normandie's on-board service.

A sterling silver cocktail shaker given out as a prize on the Liberte in the 1950s. $450.

A sterling silver platter from the Liberte. $250.

Silver serving pieces used
aboard the Normandie
showing the CGT logo.

A tea and coffee service
from the Normandie.

A Limoges commemorative plate
issued in 1989 on the first transatlantic crossing by the former France as
the Norway. $150. There is also a cup
and saucer in the same pattern, $75.

Reverse of the plate.

China used on the United States showing the gray star pattern. Presentation dinner plates with the eagle in gold, $400; dinner plate with gray stars, $125; dessert plate, $10, and cup, $30.

A cream pitcher used on the Furness Lines in the 1930s. $55.

A presentation plate used on the S.S. United States. Notice the eagle insignia. $400.

These silver serving pieces used on the United States showing the eagle insignia range in price from $300 to $1,200. Silverware is stamped with the special shell design called Manhattan. Dinner forks, $30; lunch forks, $25; dinner knife, $40, and teaspoon $15.

A close-up of the eagle on a champagne bucket used on board the United States. $800.

Silverware from the United States, marked "US Lines 52" for the date the ship was launched. $35.

An ice tong showing the United States's Manhattan pattern. $45.

A water tumbler used on board the United States showing the U.S. eagle insignia. $45.

The complete glass service used on board the United States. A water tumbler, $45; a whiskey glass, $80; high-ball, $80; a wine glass, $100; a champagne glass, $120; a sherry glass, $100; a cordial glass, $80; a cocktail glass, $100, and a water goblet, $100.

A Wedgwood plate designed for use in the 1970s on board QE2. Today it is used in the Princess and Britannia Grills and the Caronia restaurants.

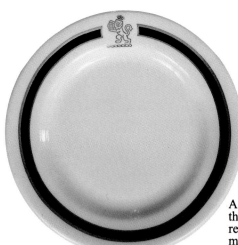

A newer version of the plate with a revised lion logo made in Norway by its new owners.

A Royal Doulton plate with the traditional Cunard lion logo used in the 1990s in QE2's Queen's Grill.

A Wedgwood mustard pot used on QE2.

A small oyster shell used on Cunard ships in the 1950s. $30.

A 1997 place setting from the Mauretania restaurant on QE2 showing the new plates made in Norway with another version of the Cunard logo. This waffled-edged plate is also used on the Royal Viking Sun and the Vistafjord.

Norwegian-made china used on the Lido deck and during tea on QE2 and the Royal Viking Sun.

Room service china from QE2, 1997.

China from the Peter Deilmann EuropAmerica riverboats with the Deilmann logo.

A porcelain Swedish America Line souvenir pitcher in the shape of a funnel sold in the 1950s. Note the three golden crowns. $90.

A 1996 plate used on the Sea Goddess.

A tourist-class November 1937 Normandie kosher menu. $50.

The other side of the menu. From the 1930s through the 1960s, most of the liners had special kosher kitchens and kosher china. The QE2 was the last to have a kosher kitchen. QE2 served kosher food through the 1980s. Today there is no kosher kitchen.

A kosher saucer stamped Cunard/White Star and used on board the Queen Mary. $50.

A kosher plate from the S.S. United States. $60.

A kosher creamer used on board the S.S. United States. $80.

Another kosher bowl from the S.S. United States. $50.

A tea cup from the Zim Lines, probably from the Shalom. $75 for cup and saucer.

Menu cover from a 1967 Passover cruise on the Shalom. $45.

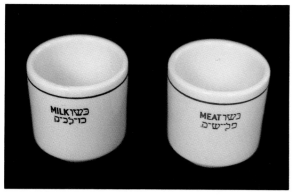

Two kosher condiment containers, one for milk, one for meat, used on board the Queen Mary. $30 each.

A kosher bowl used on QE2.

A 1989 plate from a special dining room organized and supervised by Paul Bocuse on the Royal Viking Sun. The restaurant was not a success and closed after one year. $75.

A plate from the Royal Viking Sea used in the 1980s. $75.

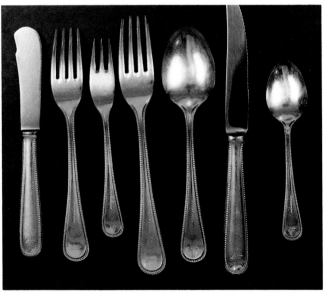

Silverware with the Royal Viking Sun sea eagle logo.

A 1997 plate from the Royal Viking Sun.

Glasses with the Royal Viking Sun's sea eagle logo.

A plate used on the Royal Viking Queen.

A Norwegian America Lines logo on a sugar bowl.

A souvenir glass bought on the Bremen. $75.

Two salt shakers with the Cunard lion logo. The older one has a gold rim on top. But after a few years all the gold rubbed off from wear so the china was redesigned with a gold stripe around the rim instead. $35 and $25.

A discontinued gold-rimmed sugar bowl
with the Cunard name under the lion. $35.

A Royal Doulton china teapot for QE2.

The creamer and the sugar
bowl.

The QE2 Wedgwood tea
service.

The Japanese service used on QE2. Since the 1990s the increase of Japanese travelers aboard Cunard ships has resulted in Japanese menus, Japanese china, and on-board Japanese speaking hostesses.

Generic china used on the Lido deck on QE2.

A Sagafjord and Vistafjord plate. $50.

The reverse of Sagafjord/Vistafjord plate.

A sugar bowl and creamer in the room service pattern used on QE2.

Chapter 6

Inside the Public Rooms

Ashtrays, Matches, Lighters, Playing Cards, and Cocktail Napkins

Meal hours have remained constant, but after-dinner options have changed considerably through the years.

Ballin was the first to establish a grand public room on board where both sexes could mingle. Until then, the only form of socialization had been found in the dining room.

Society has changed in its attitudes towards unsupervised socialization of the sexes. Before World War I, men and women were more formal in their interrelationships and more conscious of societal restraints. Traditionally, men retired after dinner to an all-male company and women would visit among themselves. In addition, large public rooms created an economic problem for the shipping lines. Unlike the cabins, they were generally not a great source of revenue.

After World War I, with the relaxing of society's mores, shipping lines began to see the advantage of their public rooms as places to socialize. Soon they were designing larger, more elaborate public rooms with gardens, palm courts, ballrooms, card rooms, and cocktail lounges.

As a result, night life became more elaborate and ships hired professional musicians and brought aboard full-scale orchestras. There were afternoon tea dances and a nightclub ambiance at night. Women dressed in long gowns, furs, and dazzling jewels. Men wore tuxedos at night and dress suits during the day.

From the 1940s through the 1960s, much of the elegance of shipboard life came from the on-board presence of celebrities. Passengers included politicians such as Winston Churchill and Vyacheslav Mikhailovich Molotov, commerce and industry leaders, and such stage and screen greats as Douglas Fairbanks, Dolores Del Rio, Elizabeth Taylor, Marlene Dietrich, Noel Coward, Mary Pickford, David Niven, Burt Lancaster, Abbott and Costello, and on and on.

On the early ships, as on land, smoking was not allowed in the dining room and special smoking rooms were set aside for after dinner cigars and cigarettes. Until the 1930s, these rooms were traditionally for men only.

Men usually retired to the smoking room after dinner, and women had access to both a reading room, a writing room, two verandahs, and a palm court.

Today as cigars have become more trendy, many ships have set up smoking rooms where men and women can indulge their love of smoking without disturbing non-smokers.

Gambling has always been one of the great diversions while at sea. The most traditional forms have always been the ship's tote, in which passengers guessed the day's mileage. Others have been a form of "horse racing," cards, bingo, or improvised games of chance.

Early White Star brochures alerted passengers to the peril of both seasickness and traveling con-men who regularly crossed the seas looking for easy prey. "All ship passengers are treated free by the ship's doctor and all related medicines are also provided free," said the brochure.

Passengers were also advised that "certain persons, believed to be professional gamblers, are in the habit of traveling to and fro in Atlantic steamships. In bringing this to the knowledge of travelers, the Managers, while not wishing in the slightest degree to interfere with the freedom of action of patrons of the White Star Line, desire to invite their assistance in discouraging games of chance, as being likely to afford these individuals special opportunities for taking unfair advantage of others."

On a recent trip aboard the Royal Viking Sun, one of the more popular afternoon activities was the bingo game. Cards sold for five dollars apiece and lucky passengers could win up to $200 for the grand prize. The casino manager told us that committed slot machine gamblers spend as much as $3,000 a day.

On a 1924 Mediterranean cruise aboard the Cunard/White Star ship the S.S. Scythia, an independent tour operator ran the sightseeing tours. Brochures advertised "five passengers to a private car with stops in Palestine, Egypt, Spain, and Greece." Another brochure cautioned that an evening arrival at Constantinople could be hazardous, "Cruise members are respectfully advised not to land, as it is not very safe, especially for ladies, and there is nothing to see."

A 1959 Queen Elizabeth daily program included shuffleboard, deck tennis, deck quoits, bridge, canasta, chess, Turkish baths, table tennis, and fancy headdress competitions.

During the 1940s and 1950s, there was access to Voice of America and BBC broadcasts.

Today QE2 reflects a new Europe. Evening entertainment includes an assortment of British-American dancers, singers, and comedians. Daily entertainment includes lectures by BBC correspondents, retired ambassadors and public officials, art historians, authors, and even concerts by groups such as an all-male singing chorus from Scotland and Wales. In addition to current movies, there will be theatrical readings by British and American actors.

Most ship cabins are equipped with television with regular CNN broadcasts, and there are video libraries. German ships such as the Peter Deilmann Line, transmit English movies in the cabins each night for their English-speaking clientele.

In addition, there are still traditional shipboard sports such as shuffleboard, a roped-in golf driving range, skeet shooting, and an outdoor and indoor swimming pool.

On Mediterranean, Caribbean, or East Asian itineraries, many passengers prefer to spend their days on deck lazily reading, relaxing, or just sunning themselves.

Reading remains the most popular on deck activity and ship libraries are stocked with an enormous selection of fiction, nonfiction, and, whenever possible, with the latest newspapers.

On a 1997 transatlantic crossing on QE2, the librarian commented that each morning the on-board library processed more books daily than do most on-land metropolitan libraries. And it is common to see all the chairs, sofas, and desks filled with avid readers using the reference materials.

Jogging has become so popular within recent years that many ships have set up a fast-jogging lane and special jogging hours so joggers will not interfere with the more leisurely walkers.

Since its recent highly publicized "refit" in 1996, QE2 has taken on a new informality to broaden its appeal to a younger clientele. Not only are the cabins brighter and more modern, with larger closets, but the public rooms—the lounges, the bars, the grand ballrooms—have more pizazz, with mirrors, glass, and sparkling crystal ornaments.

Seasickness has always been the bane of seagoing travelers, but with new and improved stabilizers, this is seldom the problem it was years ago. Today most ships are equipped with the latest in seasick prevention remedies. In the early 1970s, ship stewards would provide passengers with carefully wrapped packets of crackers and saltines. Today, ship personnel carry medical patches or crystallized ginger.

On a recent cruise on the Bergen Line mail steamer MS Richard With, fellow passengers comforted each other with crackers when a sudden sea squall in the North Sea produced twenty foot waves, causing passengers to do quick sidesteps across decks, going from chair to chair for support.

Religion has always been part of the seagoing week. Services are held Sundays and holidays. QE2 boasts that it has the only on-board fully equipped Jewish synagogue.

Among the most popular shipboard collectibles are ashtrays, matches, lighters, playing cards, cocktail napkins, invitations, daily programs, and party favors such as the paper sailor hats and the gala ribbons given out at the farewell dinner.

Years ago, the public room or grand lounge was the heart of ship life. During the day it was filled with entertainment such as fashion shows, lectures, bingo, and readings. At night it became a ballroom and the scene of dancing, nightclub revues, magicians, masquerade balls, and games. Many people still treasure trophies and gifts from at-sea competitions.

Trophies are coveted collectibles. The Liberte gave out silver cocktail shakers. The France gave out miniature models. The Italian Line gave out medals.

Another collectible is the gala ship ribbon given out at the farewell dinners. These small grosgrain ribbons had the ship's name embroidered on them.

In later years, other lines would offer passengers small tokens and travel incentives. The Vistafjord gave out Skald pins and individual itinerary ashtrays made by Rosenthal China.

It was common for first-class passengers to travel with their dogs. Many ships had "dog walks," "pet menus," and dog walkers. The Duke and Duchess of Windsor always walked their own dogs when crossing the Atlantic. Illustration. $25.

Standing at the rail at sea. Illustration. $25.

Deck stewards serving tea or bouillon to passengers. Steamer "rugs" or blankets and deck chairs are among the many classic collectibles. There have been many modern reproductions of the traditional wooden deck chair. Illustration. $50.

Scarlet lacquered wooden deck chairs with cushion from the Normandie used on the tourist-class promenade. $3,450. Beechwood folding deck chair from the Ile de France. $1,380.

"Sea Legs," a 1931 book on ship-board life by Oliver Herford. $35.

A brushed aluminum folding deck chair with red webbing and a champagne-color blanket with the United States logo. This chair usually sells for $1,000. In 1995 it went for $5,000 at the Christie's auction. It was manufactured by the Troy Sunshade Company in Troy, New York and was used on the promenade deck. A lighter and smaller one with rubber straps was used around the swimming pool. $425.

Daily games of croquet, tennis, and golf, modified for ship play, were common activities on ships, weather permitting. Illustration. $10.

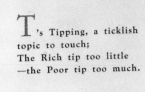

An illustration from "Sea Legs." Tipping is part of the ocean-going experience for both passengers and crew. $10.

An illustration from "Sea Legs" showing a passenger working out on the "electric horse." Illustration. $10.

A 1894 hand-colored music program cover used on the S.S. Amerika. $40.

Another 1894 music program used on the S.S. Amerika. $40.

A pre-World War I program of music played aboard Cunard ships. $35.

A tissue case to blot lipsticks, used aboard the French Line. $35.

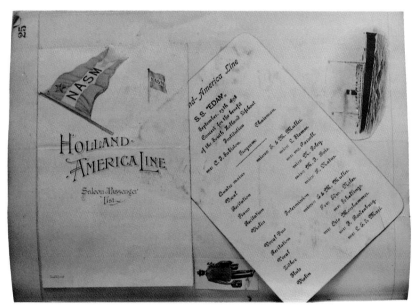

A 1898 musical benefit program for dining saloon passengers aboard the S.S. Edam. $35.

R.M.S. "QUEEN ELIZABETH"

"WHO SAID THIS" QUIZ

1 Speak softly and carry a big stick ....
2 To the victors belong the spoils ....
3 I never saw a man I didn't like ....
4 Go West young man, go West ....
5 A sucker is born every minute ....
6 I'd rather be right than President ....
7 Handsome is as handsome does ....
8 Ask me no questions and I'll tell you no fibs ....
9 The pink of perfection ....
10 War is hell ....
11 Enough is as good as a feast ....
12 Let all live as they would die ....
13 The way to a man's heart is through his stomach ....
14 Bread is the staff of life ....
15 To thine ownself, be true ....
16 The proof of the pudding is in the eating ....
17 Cut off your nose to spite your face ....
18 I have not begun to fight ....
19 Poverty makes strange bedfellows ....
20 I kiss the dear fingers so toil worn for me ....

A prize will be awarded for the first correct or nearest correct solution received at the Purser's Bureau. The competition will be closed at 5.00 p.m., today, and the winning entry, together with the key solution, will be posted on the Notice Board outside the Purser's Bureau at 6.00 p.m.

Passenger's Name ....

Room No. ....   Time handed in ....

No. 3

A Queen Elizabeth passenger competition. $5.

R.M.S. "QUEEN ELIZABETH"
Passenger List Competition
AUTHORITY: CHAMBERS'S DICTIONARY

The following clues represent surnames which appear in the Passenger List.

A prize will be awarded for the first correct or nearest correct solution received at the Purser's Office.

The competition will be closed at 5.00 p.m. today and the winning entry, together with the key solution, will be posted on the Notice Board outside the Purser's Office at 6.00 p.m.

1   Said to rotate the world   ....

2   A weight lifter   ....

3   Ball game played mostly in Ireland   ....

4   Sounds as though a writing instrument has been retrieved   ....

5   There are 52 to one   ....

6   Most famous house in America   ....

7   Bloodless object, so they say   ....

8   A crossing, but not the Atlantic   ....

9   Sly bacon   ....

10   Sounds like a grandmother imposter   ....

11   Different years   ....

12   Get your eye in Mr. !   ....

13   Well-known code   ....

14   Type of tax   ....

15   Associated with 1066 and all that   ....

16   Large sea fish   ....

17   Add saint for a famous eighteen   ....

18   What this means how much   ....

19   A draw-back   ....

20   Black or white you are limited to moving a square laterally and one diagonally   ....

Passenger's Name   ....

Room No................   Time handed in ....

FIRST CLASS

A Queen Elizabeth passenger list competition. Passengers had to find answers to the clues by using names found in the passenger list. $10.

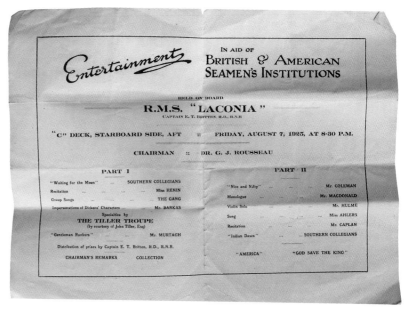

A 1925 entertainment program used aboard the Laconia. $10.

Two 1962 daily programs of events aboard the Mauretania and the Queen Mary, $10 each.

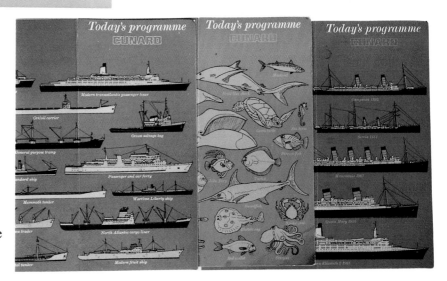

Daily programs from the Queen Elizabeth. $10.

Another Cunard program cover. $10.

A Royal Viking Sun musicale program. $5.

The Observation Lounge and Cocktail bar on the Queen Mary. Note the black and white Queen Mary ashtrays on the tables and on the bar. $100-$150 each.

The black and white ashtray used on Queen Mary. There are two versions, one is labeled Queen Mary, $150, the other Cunard, $100-$130.

A black cigarette lighter with the name Queen Mary in white letters. This lighter also came in white with black letters. Black and white were considered very chic colors. In fact the Verandah Grill was covered with a black carpet. $90.

Post-World War II Cunard matches. $10.

The smoking room on Royal Viking Sun, 1997.

The Sagafjord is no longer flying the Cunard flag. Cunard is moved its head-quarters from New York City to Miami, Florida on November 28, 1997. Matchbooks used on Cunard ships in the 1990s. $3 each.

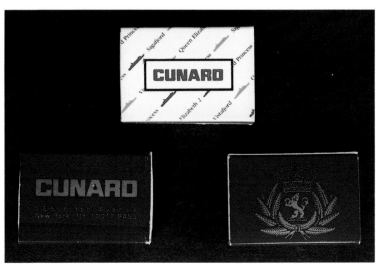

Chapter 7

Shipboard Festivities

Invitations, Games, Gala Ribbons, Party Hats, Certificates, and Tambourines

Sitting on deck has always been one of the most relaxing ways to pass a day at sea. A French Line brochure advertised "a dream-blue sky in your deck chair. Feast your sea appetite with the world-famed French cuisine. Wrap yourself in a sea breeze and relax."

Until the 1980s, one of the first chores for a passenger was reserving a table in the dining room and then reserving a deck chair.

On the earliest ships, sturdy wooden park benches were bolted along the insides of the ship deck. Gradually these were replaced by individual seats that were installed on the deck and deck stewards would reserve the seat by inserting each passenger's name into a brass insert.

Since so much time was spent sitting on deck or visiting in public rooms, smooth sailing with no tilt was an important selling point for ships. Two Cunard ships, the 1874-75 Umbria and Etruria, were known affectionately by their officers as the submarines because they dived into the waves instead of mounting them.

One of the biggest advances in shipboard life was the introduction of a promenade deck, which was supposed to provide not only an exercise area but a shelter against the weather. The first promenade deck appeared on the Oceanic in 1871 and Cunard brochures still stress the restorative nature of an ocean crossing.

As a footnote, Olympic first-class passengers complained of being splashed with ocean spray at the bow as they walked along the promenade deck, so White Star chairman Bruce Ismay ordered a glass enclosure over Titanic's forward promenade deck. This feature is the only way to distinguish pictures of Titanic from the Olympic.

The Germans were among the first to stress exercise and good physical well-being aboard ship. Health clubs and swimming pools soon became part of a luxury ship's design. It is interesting to note that it was the Cunard line that established the daily regimen of walking around the deck. Even today, German liners still only have limited promenade decks while on QE2 it is possible to walk completely around the deck in one complete lap.

Doing a daily lap around the deck has not only been a part of the oceangoing life, but an antidote against cabin fever. Passengers would dress warmly, bracing themselves for the invigorating air of the Atlantic winds. It took eight laps around to cover a mile on the Queen Mary for walkers such as the Duke and Duchess of Windsor, who walked their dogs regularly at sea. Passengers on the Royal Viking Sun, where four laps make a mile, or on the Vistafjord, earn Golden Door credits and prizes for toting up mileage.

A 1962 Queen Mary brochure offered "Keep-fit hours for ladies" and another series for gentlemen.

Other improvements on board included larger cabins, larger portholes to bring in more light, and electric bells to summon deck stewards, a vast improvement over the earlier practice of having the passengers leave their room to shout for help or service.

Later ships have always stressed recreation. The Ile de France had its own miniature golf course located on top of the cargo hatch. The Normandie had a full-size tennis court in the area between its two funnels.

Some of the earliest deck games were ladies-only "potato races," "egg-and-spoon races," "shoe races," and "nail driving contests." For the gentlemen there were "thread and needle races" and "cock fighting."

It is hard to imagine these elegant transatlantic dignitaries indulging in such games as the Whistling Game, in which the man would run to his partner, drink a glass of soda, eat a biscuit, and then whistle a tune, challenging his partner to try and guess the tune.

Another shipboard pursuit was a nail-driving contest for ladies, who would run to a plank, hammer in two nails, and return to the starting point.

More traditional activities would be deck tennis, shuffleboard, mahjong, and, for the men, boxing and blindfold races.

Family activities included potato races, sack races, and a shipboard specialty, the suitcase game. The trick was to race across the deck, open a suitcase, unpack it, put whatever was on the deck back inside, and race back across the deck.

Another game of similar innocence was one popular on the French Line. The contestant would have to thrust an empty whiskey bottle upright on the deck using a shuffle board stick.

Beginning in the 1970s and on through the present, the most popular activities would be card playing, bingo, and scavenger hunts, fancy dress balls, musicales, and concerts. Until the 1930s, there were few professional entertainers and the crew would put on new uniforms and play instruments once off duty.

Cunard hired its first professional twelve-piece orchestra for the Caronia. Until then it often hired collegiate musicians from Ivy League colleges such as Yale, Harvard, and Princeton. Other entertainments would be fancy dress parades and strolling minstrels.

The 1971 daily program on Queen Elizabeth 2 offered Roman Catholic services at 9:30 a.m., Protestant services at 10 a.m., a Divine service at 11 a.m., golf lessons on deck, trap shooting, shuffleboard, bingo, and an evening of the Roaring Twenties in which the suggested dress was shift dresses, feathers, and boas for the women, and blazers, boaters, and mustaches for the gentlemen.

A 1970s series of gift shop matches show the different Cunard ships. $20.

More ship matches. $5. In years to come these, too will become collectibles. In the past few years, Canadian Pacific pre-World War I matches have sold for $25, Ile de France matches for $20, and Queen Mary pre-War wooden matches for $20.

An ashtray used on Hapag Lloyd ships showing the colors of the ship's funnels. The funnels are still painted the same colors today. $35.

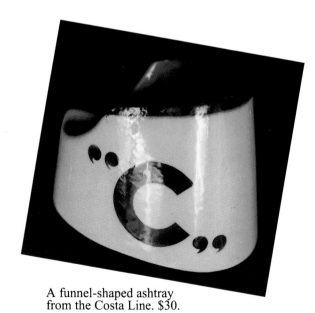

A funnel-shaped ashtray from the Costa Line. $30.

An ashtray sold in the gift shop of the Europa. $25.

A bronze ashtray of the Normandie designed by H. Balzon, probably sold in Le Havre. $75.

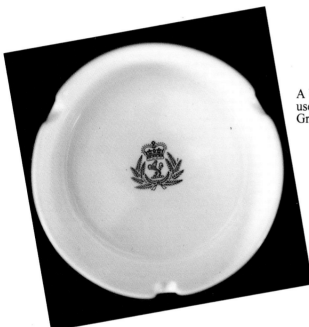

A Wedgwood ashtray used in the Queen's Grill on QE2.

Three of the four shapes of glass ashtrays used on the United States. $35.

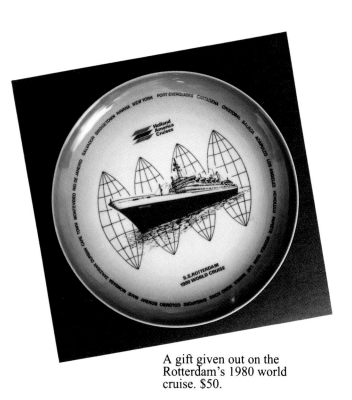

A gift given out on the Rotterdam's 1980 world cruise. $50.

A glass ashtray used on the Royal Viking Sun with the sea eagle logo. $25.

A Holland America Rotterdam ashtray in the blue Delft pattern. $50.

An "opalex" ashtray made in France for the Italian line with the words "North America" on one side and "South America" on the other. $60. Jean Luce designed a similar-style ashtray for the French Line and the Normandie, $90.

An Italian Line lighter sold aboard. $45.

A souvenir porcelain ashtray sold on the Andrea Doria during the years 1953–55. $150.

A souvenir porcelain ashtray sold on the Cristoforo Columbo and the Andrea Doria during the years 1953–1955. $150.

A souvenir ashtray sold on the Conte Biancamano in the 1950s. $150.

A souvenir sold on the Leonardo da Vinci in 1961. $150.

A crackled glaze ashtray used on the Normandie in 1935. $50.

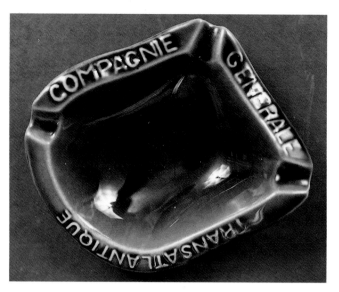

A green ceramic ashtray used on the French Line in the 1930s. $50.

"The Cheminee qui fume," an ashtray used on the France. The smoke comes out through the funnel when a cigarette is laid in the cigarette rest. This ashtray came in four colors. $250.

A glass ashtray used on the France. $40.

Two ashtrays used on the France. $30 each.

An Ile de France ashtray, $50, and a Conte di Savoia ashtray, $150.

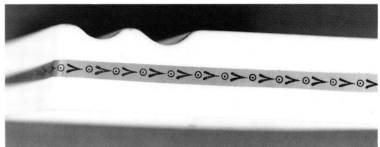

Notice the pre-War logo of "O's" and "V's" used on Conte di Savoia ashtray. This logo is found on other Italian Line items.

A glass American Hawaii Cruises ashtray. $35.

A Swedish America Line ashtray with the logo of three gold crowns. $35.

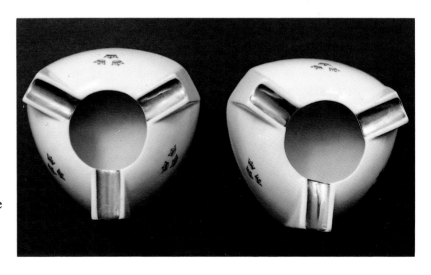

A glass Swedish America Line ashtray with the three crowns logo. $25.

A bone china ashtray used on Hamburg American liners in the 1930s. $65.

A Carnival Lines souvenir ashtray for the Mardi Gras, the Carnivale, and the Festivale. $35.

An ashtray from the Zim Lines. $35.

A Norwegian America Shipping Line ashtray, $25; a Greek Line ashtray, $20; an opalex ashtray by Jean Luce used on the Normandie, $90, and a North German Lloyd ashtray, $30.

A souvenir sold on the Queen Elizabeth 2 in the 1970s. $30.

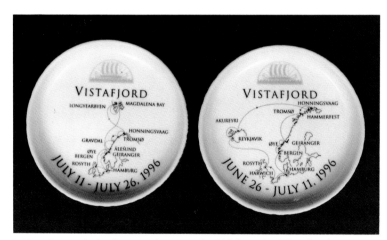

Two Rosenthal ashtrays given out in 1996 on the Vistafjord. $15 each.

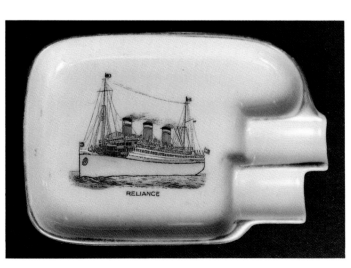

A pink plastic ashtray used on the outside decks of the Sea Goddess. $20.

A souvenir ashtray sold on the Reliance, comes in at least two sizes. $40.

Royal Viking Sun's cocktail napkins. $1.

S.S. United States playing cards, $60,
Holland America Line cards, $30; and
cards from the Home Lines, $25.

Two Cunard cocktail napkins from QE2. $1.

Two sets of 1950s Cunard
playing cards, $40 each, and
one from the Italian Line, $35.

Playing cards from the Liberte. $40.

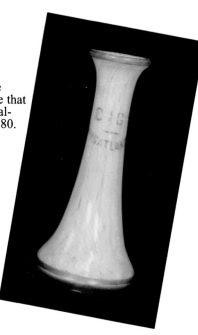

A vase used on the Compagnie Generale Transatlantique. Note that the design ensured balance in rough seas. $80.

A vase with the Cunard lion logo used on QE2. $30.

Two carafes with the Cunard lion logo found in the bars on the Vistafjord to hold nuts. $30.

Two carafes used on QE2 in the 1990s. This style is no longer in use but was part of a new advertising campaign when Trafalger House took over the management of Cunard in the 1970s. $50 each.

Two carafes used on the Royal Viking Sun to hold nuts. $30 each.

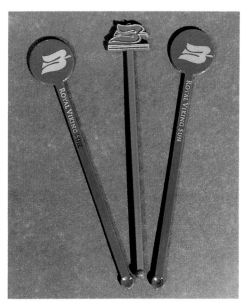

Swizzle sticks found in the bar on the Royal Viking Sun. $1 each.

A certificate of merit given to all passengers participating in masquerade parades aboard the United States. $10.

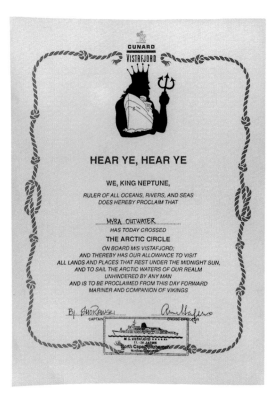

A certificate given out to passengers crossing the Arctic Circle aboard the Vistafjord. $10.

An invitation to cocktails in the Officers' Wardroom on the QE2. $10.

A certificate to all passengers crossing on the thirtieth anniversary of QE2's launch. $10.

A cup given away during team trivia on the Royal Viking Sun. $5.

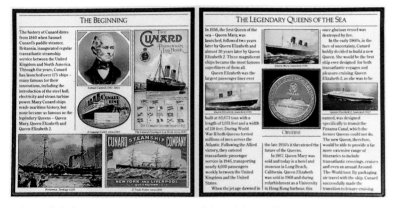

A medal given out as a memento of the 1987 maiden voyage of the "new" QE2 after its refit. $50.

A 1997 World cruise memento from QE2. $15.

A plate given out to 1996 QE2 world cruise passengers. $50.

A souvenir from Captain John Burton Hall of the QE2.

127

A wooden party tambourine used on the Cristoforo Colombo in 1954. $45.

A Queen Elizabeth maiden voyage medal. $100.

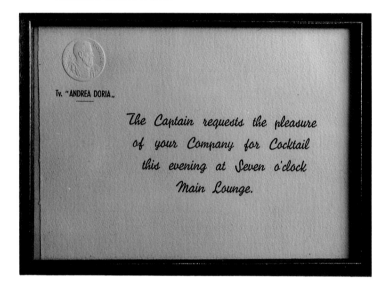

An invitation for cocktails from the Captain of the Andrea Doria. $85.

This QE2 bell is displayed on QE2 on Two Deck, D stair landing, and is used once a year on QE2 as a punch bowl for a New Year's Day reception and whenever requested as a baptismal fount.

Invitations for cocktails from the Captain and the Golden Door Spa as well as the cards announcing time changes aboard the Royal Viking Sun. $5 each.

Plastic party tambourines used on the Raffaello in 1969. $25 each.

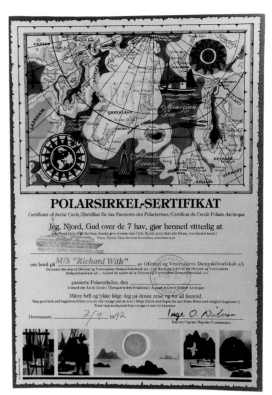

A certificate given to passengers on the Bergen Line's Richard With after crossing the Arctic Circle. $10.

A paper party hat used on the France in 1974. Since these are so fragile, few have survived. $50.

A gala party ribbon given out on the maiden voyage of the French Line's Liberte. The Liberte was formerly the German ship the Europa. $60.

Gala ribbons given out at the farewell dinners on the Andrea Doria and the Lusitania. $150 and $60.

More gala ribbons. $60 each.

Days pass into each other on a world cruise. The Royal Viking Sun changes the mat in the elevators daily as a way of keeping track of each day. Someday this too will be a collectible.

A 1930s Neptune's Proclamation given out to passengers after crossing the Equator on the Columbus. $35.

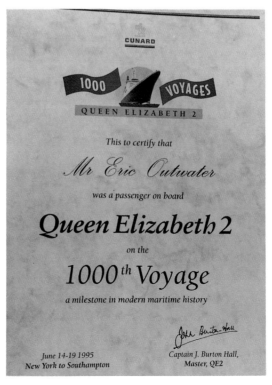

A certificate given out to passengers on Queen Elizabeth 2's thousandth voyage. $10.

Gift Items

Bottles, Commemorative Plates, Compacts, Models, Toys, Medallions, Medals, and Pins

One of the most popular sources of ship stuff has always been the on-board gift shop. Compacts, silver pillboxes, pens, perfumes, small models, souvenir ashtrays, pens, dolls, and penknives are only a few of the collectibles sold as gifts on board. Cunard used to sell copies of its own china in the gift store and mark it "souvenir" to counteract the common practice of pilfering the service used on board.

Cunard sold very high quality items such as enamel compacts and bone china. Ship models were popular items in the gift shops as well as Norah Wellings' sailor dolls.

Ashore many manufacturers realized the appeal of ship models and liquor companies began to produce a series of specialty bottles in the shape of the great liners. Candy and biscuits were also sold in tins with the ships pictured on the front. The Queen Mary was most often pictured on biscuit tins. The French and the Germans also capitalized on marketing their ships. Shops in the port city of Le Havre always stocked ship souvenirs especially those with the likeness of the Normandie.

Since fathers and sons have always bonded with ships and sailing, there have been many children's games, puzzles, and models of ships manufactured in America and abroad.

Other popular collectibles have been pens, knives, etched glasses, souvenir ashtrays, postcards, and teddy bears. One of the biggest challenges for collectors has been identifying authentic articles sold aboard and those collectibles produced years later.

Since ships such as the Titanic, the Normandie, and the Queens have always captured the imagination of the public, they have been reproduced in many sizes and materials.

A snow dome perpetual calendar made in France with a generic ship. When you shake it snow falls over the ship. $125.

A souvenir wine tasting spoon used on the Ascania. $65.

A crystal glass made by Stuart Glass as a souvenir for the Queen Elizabeth's maiden voyage. $150.

The bronze maiden voyage medallion for the Queen Mary. $300.

Maiden voyage bronze medallions for the Normandie, $300 ($500 with original box), L'Atlantique, $350, and the Colombie post-war following a re-fit, $100.

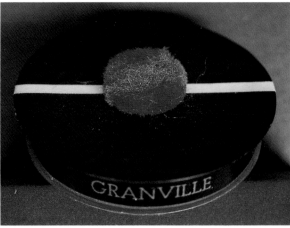

A Granville paper sailor hat filled with nylon stockings. $35.

A silver pill box sold on the Hamburg Amerika's Prinzessin Victoria Luise. $145.

A silk handbag given out to passengers dining in the Ritz restaurant on the Amerika. $150.

A silver and enamel perfume bottle sold on the North German Lloyd Line's Europa in the 1930s. $225.

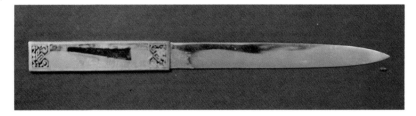

A penknife sold on the Europa. $125.

A silver napkin ring souvenir sold on the Majestic in the 1920s. $65.

An American Line biscuit tin. $100 ($300 if in mint condition)

A Normandie cookie tin, $400. There are two other more elaborate Normandie cookie tins that we have seen that replicate the ship in three dimensions and another with a more detailed painting. One sells for $1,200, the other has been priced at $2,500.

A pre-war Queen Mary cookie tin, 1936–39. $55.

A side view of the Queen Mary cookie tin showing various ships of the Cunard fleet.

Another style of Queen Mary cookie tin. $40.

A United States cookie tin. $45.

Another Queen Mary cookie tin. $35.

Another United States cookie tin. $45.

A 1969 Queen Elizabeth 2 maiden voyage cigarette tin. $95.

A Queen Elizabeth 2 candy tin sold on board in 1997. $35.

A 1930s flag used in the offices of Hamburg South America Line. $90.

Two souvenir pennants for the Queen Mary and the Queen Elizabeth. $50 each.

A plate showing the Boston Mail steamers. It is unknown whether or not this plate was used on board. It is cracked but still important because it is so rare. $300. We also found a Minton bone china Cunard commemorative plate of the Mauretania, marked Cunard Steamship Company. With a crack it sold for $65.

A souvenir plate of an 1890s steamer. $100.

A souvenir plate for the S.S. South America, a Georgian Bay Line ship. $45.

A small miniature bronze bell from the N.K.Y.'s Asama Maru given to special friends or passengers, probably on the ship's maiden voyage on October 10, 1928. $80.

A souvenir plate sold on the Queen Mary on her maiden voyage. $65.

A souvenir demitasse cup and saucer sold on the Bremen. $65.

One in a series of souvenir plates sold on the American Line ships in milk glass ribbon plate trimmed with gold rosettes. This one is of the Amerika. Another was the St. Paul. $225.

A pre-war bone china souvenir plate sold on the Swedish America Line. $95.

Post-war compacts sold on these ships. $65-200.

A sleek, modern-style compact sold on the Mauretania, post-war. $150.

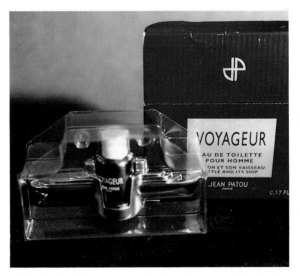

A limited edition perfume by Jean Patou with a bottle in the shape of the Normandie. Issued after the launch in 1936. Since then there have been many reproductions. This is one of the few souvenirs for men and was offered in the 1980s. $65.

This was contemporary reproduction by Jean Patou of the original Normandie perfume created in 1935, issued in a limited edition of one thousand bottles. $200.

The certificate for each of the limited edition bottles, numbered on the back.

The original Normandie perfume bottle has sold at auction for $4,830. A molded metal scent bottle created by Louis Sue, circa 1935, for Jean Patou of Paris-France.

A Bloomingdale's special of Normandie eau de toilette by Jean Patou. $75.

A souvenir pre-World War I pocket knife sold on the Bremen. $125.

A souvenir pocket knife sold on the Queen Elizabeth. $80.

The other side of the Queen Elizabeth knife.

A souvenir pocket knife sold on the Queen Mary. $125.

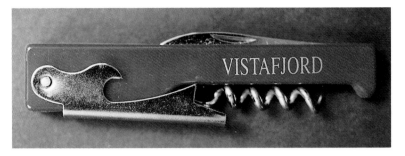

A souvenir sold on the Vistafjord in 1995. $20.

A Meissen statue of a sailor with the name Britannic on his cap. $125.

A Canoe perfume bottle in the shape of a French Line sailor. $50.

A series of liquor bottles in the shape of the Titanic and the Queen Mary. The Titanic is a souvenir of the 1970s. The Mary bottle was commissioned in 1968 by the City of Long Beach, California, where the Queen Mary is now docked permanently as a hotel. $100 each.

A souvenir bottle commissioned in 1962 to celebrate the maiden voyage of the France. $200. A smaller version was also issued, $100.

A ceramic liquor bottle in the shape of the Michelangelo sold on board the Michelangelo and Raffaello in 1965/1970. $225.

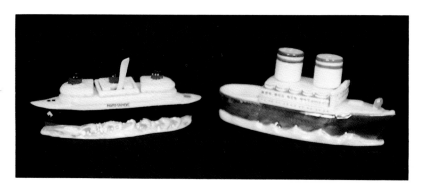

Two condiment sets in the shape of the Normandie and the Europa. $100 for the Europa and $250 for the Normandie.

A bottle of Scotch whiskey sold on QE2. $50.

A cotton handkerchief sold on all the ships of the Italian Line in the 1950s. $100.

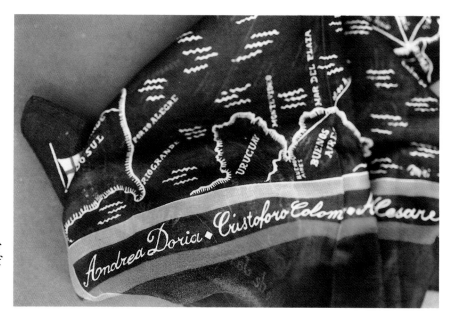

A pre-war souvenir from the Queen Mary in a plaster-like material sold on the gift shop. It still says Cunard White Star. $125.

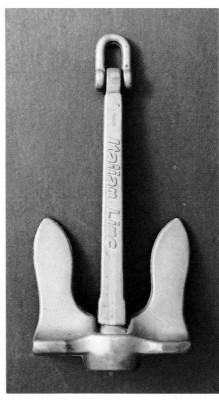

A souvenir anchor sold on board the Andrea Doria. $200.

A souvenir leather life-preserver from the Andrea Doria. $500.

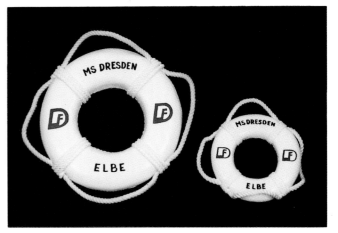

Two souvenir life-preservers sold on the Peter Deilmann's Dresden. $15 each.

A bronze model of QE2 sold on board in the 1980s. $50.

A souvenir cigarette case sold on the Royal Mail Highland Princess in the 1950s. $60.

An enamel lighter sold on the Michelangelo and the Raffaello, 1965–1970. $50.

A 1939 souvenir butterfly backed pin of the first Mauretania. $50.

A paperweight sold on the Homeric. $50.

A Candy dish given out to all 1994 QE2 World Cruise passengers. $250.

A Wedgwood teapot given out to 1993 World Cruise passengers. $250.

A QE2 commemorative plate sold on QE2 1997. $40.

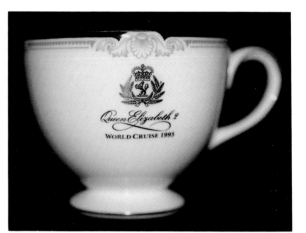

The teapot came with four teacups. $50 each.

A Wedgwood ashtray designed for QE2. $35.

Crystal highball glasses sold on QE2 in 1997. $45 each.

A 1950s souvenir butterfly wing lined ashtray sold on the Mauretania. $100.

White Star Line enamel and silver pre-World War I pin sold on the Baltic. $50.

A thousandth voyage QE2 pin, $10; a pin of the first Mauretania, $25, and a Normandie pin issued at her launch, $35.

A pin given out at the United States auction held 1984 in Norfolk, Virginia. $10.

A QE2 badge for the crew's cars. $200.

Three souvenir spoons for the Lusitania, Aquitania, and Berengaria sold onboard in the 1900s. $85 each.

A series of pins of the White Fleet. $25 each.

The Royal Viking Sun's gift shop in 1997.

Chapter 9

Dolls

Norah Wellings and
Other Doll Makers

One of the most famous sailor doll makers was the English-woman Norah Wellings. Wellings' felt ocean liner dolls became popular souvenirs of the great ocean liners of the 1930s through the 1950s. These dolls were sold aboard ship and in onshore shops. The sailors come in two styles—a grinning sailor with protruding ears and pointed feet and a smiling sailor with velvet feet and flat ears. In addition to sailors, Wellings created soldiers, airmen, and exotic South Sea islanders.

Wellings worked as a doll designer for the Chad Valley Toy Company for six years until 1926 when she opened her own factory in Shropshire, England. From 1926 through the early 1950s she continued to make dolls out of soft velvet and mark them either on the foot, on their back, or on their wrists with her label. These labels were either black, blue, or beige.

It is difficult to distinguish her early Chad Valley dolls from her later ones. The one difference is the presence of a label bearing her name. Wellings got the idea to sew on labels while working at Chad Valley. Chad Valley dolls are marked with a hand-sewn label.

When Wellings retired, Peggy Nisbet took over the line. Her dolls have brighter faces, more vibrant eyes, and a smile and are marked with a paper tag "Empire" under the collar.

The Queen Elizabeth and the Stella Polaris dolls were made by Norah Wellings. The Orsova is by Peggy Nisbet. Wellings dolls range in price from $90 to $150. Nisbet dolls are $60 to $70.

The difference between Wellings dolls and Nisbet dolls are in the facial details and the labeling. Wellings sewed her own labels on the feet, the backs, and the arms of her dolls. Nisbet marked hers with a paper label, "Empire."

A French bowling doll used aboard the French Line ships, $70, and a Home Lines' wire doll, $40.

A Holland America doll with a plastic face, $50, and a Peggy Nisbet doll from the Statendam, $60. These dolls have more animated faces than the Wellings' dolls.

A rare doll from the Andrea Doria, 1953-1955. $90.

A doll quintet. $90-150.

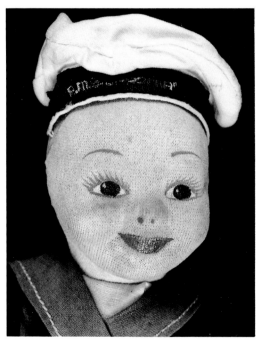

Norah Wellings' dolls come in two styles: the Stella Polaris with a grinning face and ears, and the Mauretania with a smiling face with no ears. $90-150.

147

Chapter 10

The Disaster Ships

The Maine, the Titanic, the Lusitania, the Normandie, the Morro Castle, and the Andrea Doria

Stories about the disastrous ends of the great liners have fueled the imaginations of writers, filmmakers, collectors, and school children.

When the Ile de France was sold in 1958 to Hollywood moviemakers to be sunk for the movie, "The Last Voyage," the French were outraged. She had been one of their favorite ships, and many Frenchmen found it difficult to accept that this great ship would suffer such an ignominious end as a Hollywood stage-set.

Today the movie, which starred Robert Stack and George Sanders, would have been delegated to the back shelves of video libraries, if it wasn't for the fact that many ship fans still watch the movie just to catch one more glimpse of that great liner, the Ile de France.

Although the Maine was a military ship and not an ocean liner, its sinking on February 15, 1898, in Havana harbor was one of the first ship disasters to capture the popular imagination and create an industry of souvenirs. When the ship blew up in Havana, Cuba, 260 men were killed. "Remember the Maine" became a popular war cry. The Maine was immortalized in songs, books, glassware, and candy dishes. Salvaged items were sold at a premium.

Enough has been written about the Titanic to make it the best known ocean liner of the century. While so far none of the diving expeditions have offered any of her retrieved cargo for sale, there are still many authentic Titanic souvenirs available. Many people incorrectly assume that she was sailing directly toward New York and her doom, but she made one short stop on April 11, in the Irish port of Queenstown, and several passengers disembarked.

In another irony, the Olympic collided with the HMS Hawke on September 20, 1911. The repairs to the Olympic delayed the Titanic's maiden voyage from March 20, 1912 to April 10.

One of the most fascinating authentic souvenirs is an April 11 breakfast menu that had been mailed as a postcard by one of the waiters to his wife from Queenstown. Today it is the property of the Marine Museum in Southampton, England, along with several examples of the china, Royal Crown Derby, from the a la carte dining room and Spode in the first-class dining saloon. White Star silverware used on White Star ships contemporary with the Titanic are still available. They have the White Star logo on the front and on the back are stamped with a Maltese cross. The cross was stamped on the reverse to show that this silver was sold at an approved auction.

There are two kinds of Titanic collectibles—contemporary pieces produced in the aftermath of the tragedy and modern reproductions. When dealing with Titanic items it is important to be wise and well read and understand that when it comes to the Titanic, P. T. Barnum was right, "there's a sucker born every minute." Many Titanic items are of recent origin, despite their age or patina.

The Titanic sparked an industry of mourning pictures, books, reverse glass paintings, and other souvenir items. The fascina-

tion for this ship has never stopped and with Robert Ballard's new expeditions to uncover her ocean burial place, a new line of souvenir items has been created. In 1997 there was both a Broadway musical and a movie based on the Titanic.

Coincidentally eighty-five years to the day, on April 14, 1997, QE2 passed over the Titanic's burial site. Not a single iceberg was visible anywhere in the area.

The Lusitania was the next nautical disaster to catch the popular interest. On May 7, 1915 she sank off the Head of Kinsale in Ireland. The mystery of her sinking by a German torpedo has never been solved and the small cemetery in Kinsale where her victims were buried has become a sentimental voyage for many ship buffs. Today books are still being written about whether or not the ship was carrying munitions to England.

On September 8, 1934, the Morro Castle burned at sea off the New Jersey shore on her way back from a cruise to Havana. Still burning she drifted ashore at Asbury Park, New Jersey.

The reasons for this tragedy have never been uncovered. Some suspect arson. But what is known is that for some unknown reason, the captain had turned off the ship's smoke and fire detection system on September 5, three days before the fatal fire. Two days later he was found dead in his cabin.

On the morning of the September 8, the night watchman found the first indications of fire. It has been assumed that there was an on-board explosion.

For years the survivors would hold reunions. The last one was held in 1991.

There never has been a ship that has aroused as much sentiment as the Normandie. In fact, in ship circles, it is common for people to talk about her in hushed tones. She was one of the grandest and most elegantly designed ships of the century. She created standards for on-board style that have never been surpassed.

At her launch few would have imagined that she would have come to such an ignominious fate as to be burned in New York City harbor through the carelessness of a welder trying to convert her to a troopship.

The Normandie was launched with great ceremony in 1935, almost a year late. She was the ultimate in oceangoing style. Ironically in a reaction to the fire at sea which sunk the L'Atlantique in 1933 off the English Channel, only non-combustible paneling was allowed on board and many of her public rooms such as the dining room, the smoking room, and the grand salon were sheathed in glass to make her even more fireproof.

On her seventieth voyage in August 1939, she became a prisoner of war and languished in New York harbor for two years until President Roosevelt decided to convert her to the troopship the Lafayette.

Ironically just nine years after the tragic burning of L'Atlantique, the Normandie was the victim of another fire and on February 9, 1942, the carelessness of a welder ignited one of the kapok cushions covering the walls of the grand salon and she capsized in New York harbor. It took more than eighteen months to right her and in 1946 she was sold for scrap.

Many people still remember the tragic sight of that grande dame lying on her side at Pier 88 in New York. As a footnote, my son Alexander has been a fan of the Normandie since he was eight years old and until he went to college, he would fast on February 9 in her memory. Ironically in 1985, he received a telephone call from noted marine-historian John Maxtone-Graham on that date. When Maxtome-Graham learned that Alexander was fasting he invited him into New York for tea the next month and the two sat and discussed their love of that ship and the other grand dames of the sea. For a fourteen-year-old boy that was very heady stuff and definitely an "afternoon to remember."

Probably more books have been written about the Titanic and the Normandie than about any other ships. But while Titanic items are scarce, Normandie items are expensive, and few collectors wouldn't stretch their budgets if they could to own at least one piece of these ships. In fact the Titanic and Normandie have such charisma that any sale or auction that includes Titanic or Normandie stuff is assured a crowd and financial success.

On July 26, 1956, the Italian liner the Andrea Doria collided with the Swedish American liner the Stockholm off the coast of Nantucket, Massachusetts.

To this day many collectors are stirred by the short life of this lovely Italian lady and the Stockholm, a ship that would otherwise have passed unnoticed, has achieved a new notoriety among collectors.

"A Remember the Maine" glass with an engraving of the Maine. $35.

The yellow press helped to heighten interest in the sinking of the Maine and the naval battles of the Spanish American War. Within a few months, stores were filled with an enormous variety of Maine collectibles. This musical Victorian photograph album with an enamel painting of Admiral Dewey's flagship, the Olympia, sailing into Manilla harbor on May 1, 1898, is a unique collectible. $250.

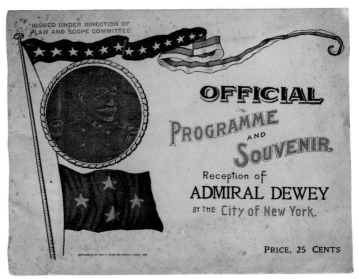

A program for a reception welcoming Admiral Dewey to New York City on September 29, 1899. $35.

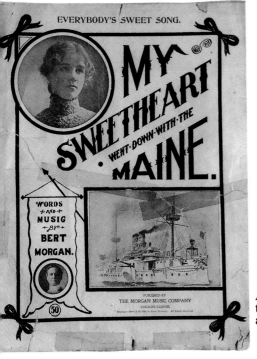

A popular song-sheet about the sinking of the Maine. $25. Later there would be songs about the Titanic and the Lusitania as well.

Above: A souvenir handkerchief with the words "U.S. Battleship Maine." $15.

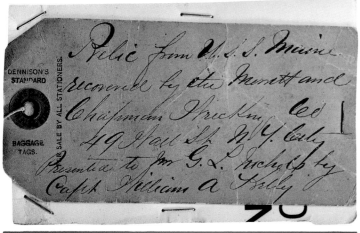

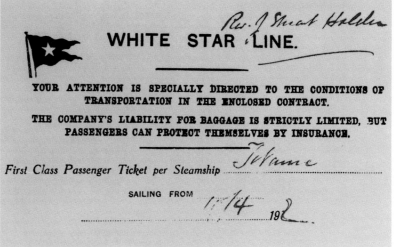

Top left: A certificate authenticating a locking "S" hook retrieved from the Maine. (See top right)

Center left: A hydraulic driven rivet from the S.S. Leviathan by United Drydocks, Inc., Fletcher Plant 1930. $200.

Bottom left: A handbill prepared by White Star publicizing the first eastbound crossing of the Titanic. The original poster sold a few years ago for $1,200. Today the price should be double.

Top right: A relic from the U.S.S. Maine. $500.

Center right: An unused first-class passenger ticket for the Titanic. Since there are so few, these are priced by the seller.

Bottom right: A restaurant ticket for dinner on board the Titanic.

A Titanic card case with original provenance. Noted ship historian Peter Boyd Smith of Cobwebs in Southampton, England, bought this from a descendant of the original crew member who took it off the ship, along with other mementos, after he learned that he had been demoted and was being sent to serve on the Olympic.

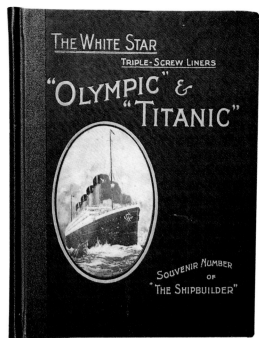

The 1911 Shipbuilder's book for the Olympic and the Titanic. The Shipbuilder is the oldest maritime publication still in existence in England. It was first published in 1906 by Albert George Hood and has published details of all the great passenger ships ever since. When this was first published it sold for two shillings, eight pence, approximately 35 cents. Today it is worth $3,500.

An unused piece of Titanic carpeting. This was part of an extra bolt of carpeting removed from the ship before she set sail to her doom.

A 1911 publicity brochure with interior views of both ships. $100.

The inside frontispiece page.

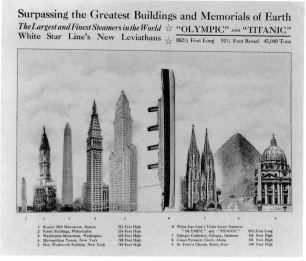

Surpassing the Greatest Buildings and Memorials of Earth
The Largest and Finest Steamers in the World ☆ "OLYMPIC" ᴀɴᴅ "TITANIC"
White Star Line's New Leviathans | 882½ Feet Long 92½ Feet Broad 45,000 Tons

Inside pages of the 1911 brochure on previous page.

Inside of an Olympic cigarette tin. Note the blackened out lines. Because the Titanic never survived her maiden voyage, all of the pictures of the Titanic were actually based on her sister ship, the Olympic.

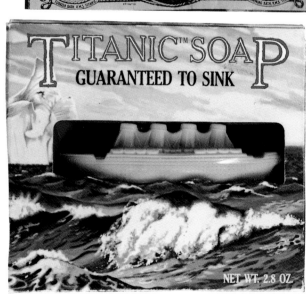

An original advertisement for Vinolia Otto Toilet Soap, the luxury soap used on the Titanic. $1,500.

A piece of Vinolia soap and its container.

An White Star cigarette tin from the 1920s showing a picture of the Olympic. It can be dated because of the presence of all the lifeboats along the side. After the Titanic went down, the rules regulating lifeboats were more strictly enforced. Originally, the builders intended to have two rows of life boats, but the final design eliminated the second row to make the boat deck wider for promenades. $2,500.

A glass money tray used on board the Olympic. $2,500.

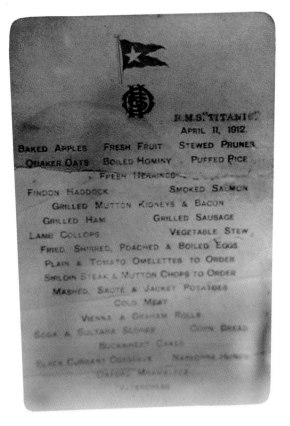

An April 11 breakfast menu mailed as a post-card by a crew member to his wife when the Titanic docked in Queenstown. (On display at the Marine Museum in Southampton, England.)

A reverse glass painting of the Titanic. $350.

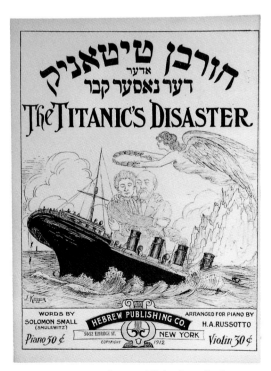

A Hebrew song sheet published on the lower East Side in 1912, celebrating the romance of the Strauses, who went down together with the Titanic. There were more than 130 songs copyrighted in America about the Titanic tragedy. $175.

Two commemorative books issued right after the sinking of the Titanic. $75 each.

A 1970s souvenir pocket knife of the Titanic. $60.

This was the last photograph taken of the Titanic off Queenstown, Ireland, by Miss Kate Odell. Her nephew Jack Odell, who was eleven years old at the time, traveled with her on the maiden voyage, disembarking at Queenstown. On April 11, 1992, the eightieth anniversary of the sinking of the Titanic, he printed limited editions of this photograph. $250.

A glass souvenir ashtray of the Olympic. $200.

A plastic glass used in the stage set of the Tony Award Broadway musical, "Titanic, the Musical." Props from the movie, "Titanic," were sold in 1997 in the J. Peterman clothing catalog. $20.

A 1970s souvenir Lusitania steward's button. $85.

A limited edition ashtray with an aerial photo taken from the French newspaper Excelsior's front page as the Normandie was leaving on her maiden voyage. $400.

The original front page of a special Normandie edition of the Excelsior newspaper, May 1935. $150.

A Normandie cookie tin from 1935–1939. $450.

A three-dimensional cookie tin sold in gift shops. Although the tin says "Normandie," it is a generic picture of a ship. $150.

An August 23, 1943 issue of Life Magazine, "The Normandie Floats Again." $75.

The commemorative medal of the Normandie's maiden voyage. $300. With the original box it is priced at $500. There was also a commemorative medal for the maiden voyage to Rio, which is not pictured. The numbers on the medal refer to the ship's tonnage. $425.

The grand salon on the Normandie.

A special limited edition commemorative plate issued in honor of the Normandie's maiden voyage. $100.

Furniture from the Normandie, which sold at Christie's in 1995 from $12,000 to $28,000 a piece.

A commemorative base metal ashtray of the Normandie showing the Statue of Liberty and the Eiffel Tower. $150.

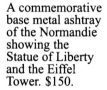

Another medal of the Normandie. These and other souvenirs were sold throughout the late 1930s and early 1940s to the ship's devoted fans. $150.

A kit to build a cut-out paper model of the Normandie. $250.

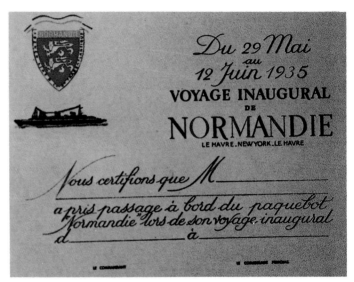

An inaugural voyage certificate from the Normandie. $900.

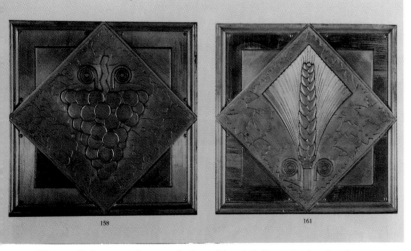

These gilt/bronze plaques designed by Adalbert Szabo for the first-class dining room of the Normandie sold for $18,000 and $21,000 at the 1995 Christie's auction in New York.

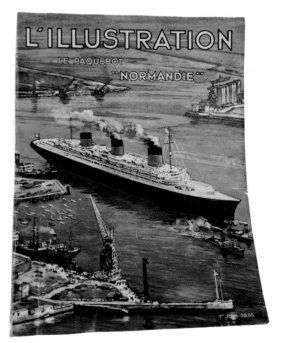

The Normandie's maiden voyage commemorative book. $150.

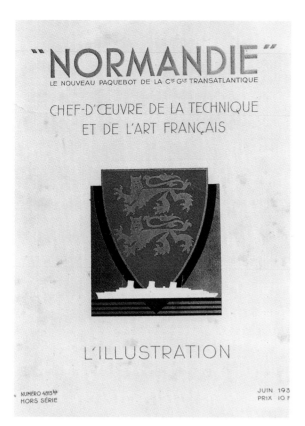

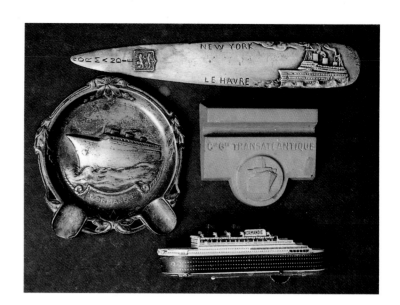

An illustrated book of the art work on the Normandie. $300.

Top right: More Normandie stuff including an ashtray, $100; a German pencil sharpener, $1,200, and a business card holder from the ship, $400; and a souvenier letter opener, $100.

Center right: A photograph of the Morro Castle taken while it burned at Asbury Park. $15.

A gala ribbon from the Andrea Doria. $150.

A gala ribbon from the Stockholm. $50.

Chapter 11

All Around the Ship

Life Jackets, Rivets, Charts

Ship collectors are indefatigable and will collect almost everything from the discarded letters from the Southampton docks to old signs used on ships, discarded doors, portholes, and any kind of paper ephemera.

When the contents of the S.S. United States were auctioned off in October of 1984 in Norfolk, Virginia, collectors and dealers arrived with trucks and vans, eager to haul off anything and everything. To this day it is still possible to buy United States china, paper ephemera, and memorabilia. One of the most prized pieces are the nineteen gold and glass panels taken from the first-class staterooms. These sell for $20,000 and up. Deck chairs can range in price from $500 to $1,200. At the 1995 Christie's auction one was sold for $5,000. Aluminum wall hangings of the eagle insignia hung on the stairwells. Today these impressive pieces sell for $3,000-5,000.

To some, collecting is an addiction, but to us it is an act of historical preservation. The age of the great liners was an age of unparalleled luxury and extravagance. While today's ships can duplicate the grandeur and elegance, none can duplicate the lifestyle. To us the passing of those ships is not only the loss of a moment of history, but the loss of an age of civility and courtesy. And our collection is a salute to those days when getting there was as much fun as being there.

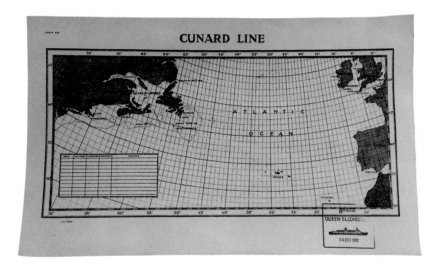

A chart from QE2. $50.

Bibliography

Archbold, Rick and Dana McCauley. *Last Dinner on the Titanic.* New York: Hyperion Press, 1997.

Bonsall, Thomas. *Titanic: The Story of the Great White Star Line Trio: The Olympic, the Titanic, and the Britannic.* New York.: Gallery Books, 1989.

Braynard, Frank O. *Picture History of the Normandie.* Mineola, New York: Dover Books, 1987.

Braynard, Frank O. and William H. Miller. *Fifty Famous Liners.* Frank O. Norton, 1982

Cox-Hunter, Jane. *Ocean Pictures: The Golden Age of Transatlantic Travel: 1936–1959.* London: Webb-Bower.

Cunard Steamship Company publication. *Triumph of a Great Tradition 1840–1990, An Official Souvenir History of the Cunard Line.* 1990.

Bruno Foucart, Charles Offrey, Francois Robichon, Claude Villers. *Normandie: Queen of the Seas.* New York, Paris: Vendome, 1985.

Eaton, John P. and Charles Haas. *Titanic: The Exhibition.* St. Petersburg, Fla.: Florida International Museum, 1997.

Herford, Oliver. *Sea Legs.* Philadelphia: J.P. Lippincott Co., 1931.

Lord, Walter. *A Night to Remember.* New York: Holt, Rinehart, and Winston, 1976.

Lord, Walter. *The Night Lives On.* New York: William Morrow and Company, 1986.

Maddocks, Melvin. *The Great Liners.* Virginia: Time-Life Books, 1978.

Maxtone-Graham, John. *Cruising and Crossing.* New York: Charles Scribner's and Sons, 1992.

Maxtone-Graham, John. *Liners to the Sun.* New York: Macmillan Publishing Company, 1985.

Maxtone-Graham, John. *Ships of State.* Ocean Liner Society, 1994.

Maxtone-Graham, John. *The Only Way to Cross.* New York: Macmillan Publishing Company, 1972.

McCart, Neil. *Atlantic Liners of the Cunard Line from 1984 to the Present Day.* England: Patrick Stephens Limited, 1990.

Miller, Bryon. *Sail, Steam, and Splendour.* New York, Times Books, 1977.

Miller, William Jr. *Crowns and Consorts: A Commemorative Journal.* 1994.

Miller, William Jr. "Encyclopedia of Ocean Liners, 1860-1994," Dover Books, New York. 1995.

Miller, William Jr. *The Fabulous Interiors of the Great Ocean Liners in Historic Photographs.* Mineola, N.Y.: Dover Publications, 1985.

Miller, William Jr. *Ocean Liners: Travel on the Open Seas.* New York: Magna Books, 1990.

Miller, William Jr. *Pictorial Encyclopedia of Ocean Liners, 1869-1994.* New York: Dover Books. 1995.

Miller, William Jr. *Transatlantic Liners, 1945-1980.* New York: Arco Publishing, Inc., 1981.

Miller, William Jr. *The Great Luxury Liners, 1927-1954.* New York: Dover Books, 1981.

Newell, Gordon. *Ocean Liners of the 20th Century.* Seattle: Superior Publishing Company, 1963.

Potter, Neil and Jack Frost. *The 'Queen Mary'.* New York: John Day Company, 1961.

Server, Lee. *The Golden Age of Ocean Liners.* New York: Smithmark Publishers, 1996.

Wall, Robert. *Ocean Liners.* New York: E.P. Dutton, 1977.

Warwick, Ronald. *QE2.* London: W. W. Norton & Co., 1993.

Warwick, Ronald and William Flayhart III. *QE2.* New York: W. W. Norton & Co., 1985.

We are also indebted to the newsletters and publications of the following organizations:

The Ocean Liner Society
1158 Fifth Avenue
New York City, 10029

The Steamship Historical Society of America, Inc.
Long Island Chapter
64 West Street
Northport, N.Y. 11768

Titanic Historical Society
P.O. Box 51053
Indian Orchard, Mass 01151-0053